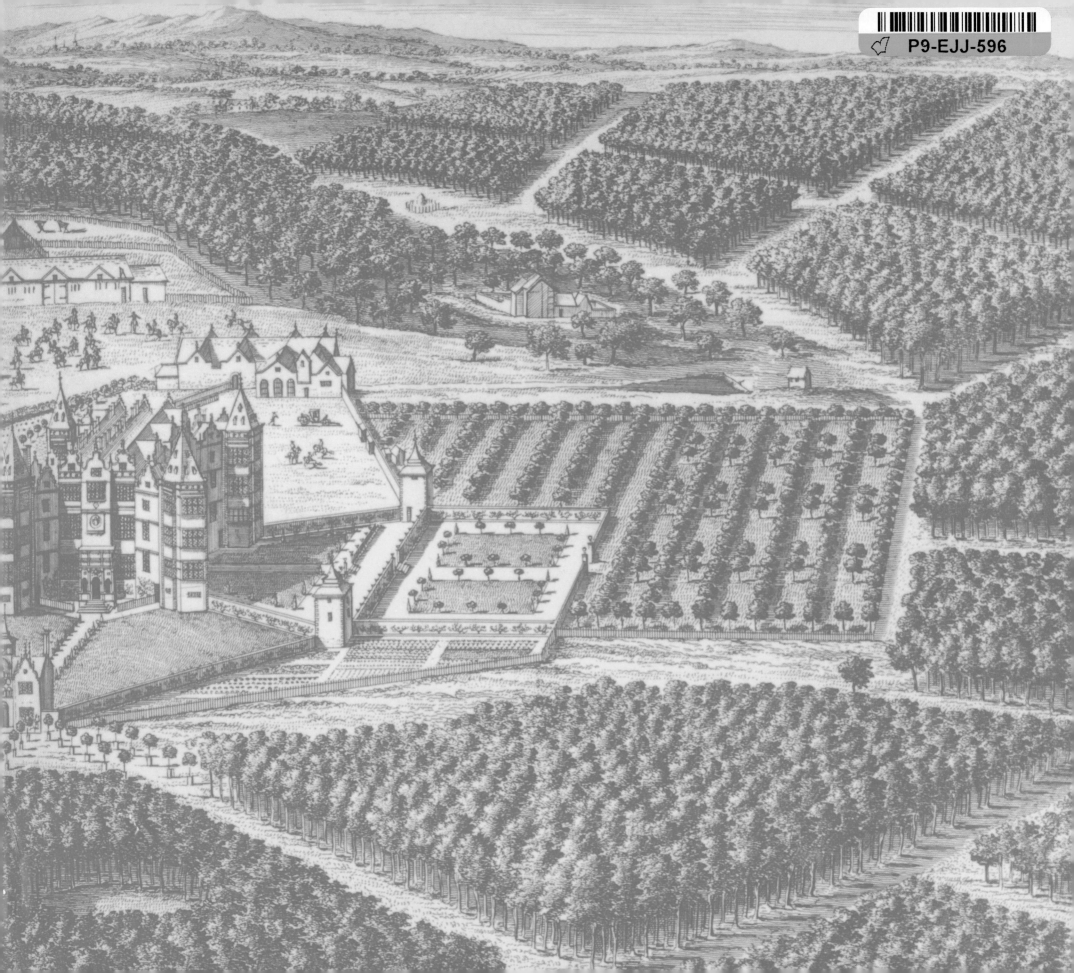

COUNTRY HOUSES
— FROM THE AIR —

COUNTRY HOUSES
—— FROM THE AIR ——

ADRIAN TINNISWOOD

PHOTOGRAPHS BY JASON HAWKES

Weidenfeld and Nicolson
London

CONTENTS

ACKNOWLEDGEMENTS
7

INTRODUCTION
8

CHAPTER ONE
LORDS OF CREATION
BLENHEIM PALACE ✦ ALTHORP ✦ KENSINGTON PALACE ✦ AUDLEY END ✦ RAGLEY HALL
KNOLE ✦ ARUNDEL ✦ BROOME PARK ✦ BADMINTON
16

CHAPTER TWO
NATURE TAMED
NEWBY HALL ✦ CHIRK CASTLE ✦ WREST PARK ✦ DYRHAM PARK ✦ HAMPTON COURT
PAINSWICK HOUSE ✦ WILTON HOUSE ✦ TEMPLE NEWSAM
48

CHAPTER THREE
PERSONAL STATEMENTS
LONGLEAT ✦ BELTON HOUSE ✦ WOLLATON HALL ✦ ASHDOWN HOUSE
BELVOIR CASTLE ✦ CHATSWORTH
76

CHAPTER FOUR
VISIONS OF ENGLAND
IGHTHAM MOTE ✦ BRYMPTON D'EVERCY ✦ WHIXLEY ✦ STANWAY HOUSE ✦ DODDINGTON HALL
GROOMBRIDGE PLACE ✦ ATHELHAMPTON ✦ PENSHURST PLACE
104

CHAPTER FIVE
FORTUNE'S WHEEL
BOARSTALL TOWER ✦ BRADGATE HOUSE ✦ UPPARK ✦ BOLSOVER CASTLE ✦ DIDMARTON MANOR
INGRESS ABBEY ✦ LEYBORNE CASTLE ✦ LULWORTH CASTLE
130

GAZETTEER
156

BIBLIOGRAPHY
158

INDEX
159

First published in 1994 by
George Weidenfeld and Nicolson Ltd
The Orion Publishing Group
Orion House
5 Upper St Martin's Lane
London WC2H 9EA

A catalogue record for this book is available from the
British Library

ISBN 0 297 83263 8

Edited by Lucas Dietrich
Designed by Bradbury and Williams
Printed and bound in Italy

*The photographic images in this book may be obtained
through the Weidenfeld and Nicolson Photographic
archive. Inquiries on telephone (0)71 498 3011, or
fax (0)71 498 0748.*

*Many other photographs taken from the air by Jason Hawkes
are available from the Jason Hawkes Aerial Collection,
telephone (0)71 486 2800.*

ILLUSTRATION SOURCES

(numbers refer to page numbers)

1, 68: Courtesy Painswick Rococo Garden Trust; 4, 8, 125:
Courtesy Athelhampton; 17, 33, 143: © English Heritage; 22,
24, 42, 96, 98-99, 124, 131, 142: Courtesy Grosvenor Prints;
24: Reproduced by kind permission of His Grace the Duke of
Marlborough/© Jarrold Publishing; 39: National Trust
Photographic Library/Angelo Hornak; 40: Reproduced by
kind permission of His Grace The Duke of Norfolk; 51, 64-5,
141: National Trust Photographic Library; 77: Yale Center for
British Art, Paul Mellon Collection; 85: The Bridgeman Art
Library; 86: National Trust Photographic Library/Mark
Fiennes; 136: Buckinghamshire County Council; 154-5: © Sir
Joseph Weld/English Heritage

ACKNOWLEDGEMENTS

FOR TRICIA LANKESTER

Many people have helped in the production of this book. My grateful thanks to them all, and in particular to colleagues and friends at the National Trust; to John Hodgson, who continues to have such good ideas; to Anthony Beeson and Iain Osborn, for their unfailing help and kindness; to Michael Dover and Lucas Dietrich, without whom the book would never have appeared at all; and to Helen, for her patience and understanding.

A T

DEDICATION

To my father for all his love and support

Jason

Athelhampton: the perfect image of the country house today.

INTRODUCTION

❖

'There is nothing quite like the English country house anywhere else in the world.' So Vita Sackville-West opened her brilliantly idiosyncratic 1941 survey, *English Country Houses*. France may have its châteaux, Italy its historic villas, Germany its 'robber castles', but, as she puts it, 'the exact equivalent of what we mean by the English country house is not to be found elsewhere'.

She was quite wrong, of course. Or at least, she was right in such an all-embracing way that the distinction doesn't count for much. There is nothing quite like the English country house in the same way that there is nothing quite like the Italian villa or the French château (or, come to that, the Irish country house or the American country house, both close cousins of our own, but both quite separate and distinct). Each is the product of a particular set of cultural forces; each is as much the creation of social history as of architectural trends, of the evolution of the landed class.

But even if we accept the difference without accepting its traditional implications – that uniqueness brings with it some sort of moral and aesthetic superiority – we are still left with a problem of definition. For Vita Sackville-West this wasn't a problem at all. The country house may be large or small, palatial or manorial, a nobleman's seat or the home of the gentry; no matter what it is, 'it possesses one outstanding characteristic: it is the English country house'. But this doesn't get us very far, nor does her qualification that 'the peculiar genius of the English country house lies in its knack of fitting in'.

Fitting in? That might hold true for Knole or

In the full splendour of its Wiltshire surroundings, Longleat still retains all the power of its sixteenth-century grandeur.

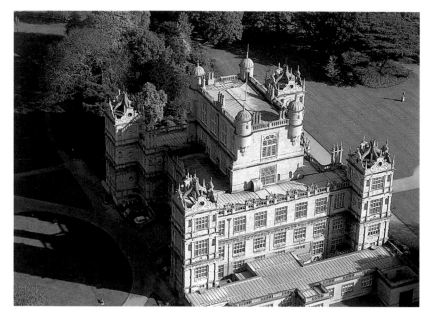

Perched atop a hill, Wollaton today conjures fairy-tale images of a long-lost time.

Ightham Mote, houses that have evolved over centuries. But did Castle Howard merge gently into its surroundings? Was Wollaton Hall a natural growth melting unobtrusively into the landscape? Hardly. Such houses were meant to be noticed, admired, marvelled at – to disrupt the landscape with their grandeur and magnificence. And if one had suggested to the Earl of Carlisle or Sir Francis Willoughby that they ought to take account of the environmental context, that Castle Howard or Wollaton should complement existing architectural patterns, they would have replied with blank astonishment. Their new houses were intended to dominate and overwhelm their surroundings in a way that makes a glass tower by Mies van der Rohe look like a country cottage with wistaria climbing the walls and roses round the door.

Let us discard the country house's 'knack of fitting in' as a defining characteristic. Along with that, let's also discard the physical and architectural attributes that Vita Sackville-West rightly dismisses. Size has to go – a small house like Whixley or Ashdown, say, would be dwarfed by the outbuildings at Blenheim or Newby, never mind the main block. So do shape, style and general appearance: any definition claiming to encompass palaces – Audley End and Chatsworth, Blenheim and Hampton Court – alongside a moated Caroline house like Groombridge Place or a rambling Tudor manor such as Athelhampton, clearly has to rely on more than looks.

So what about function? We seem to be on firmer ground here. After all, surely any and every architectural form is primarily an expression of human behaviour.

Behaviours change, however. When Sir John de Pulteney dined each day in his vast hall at Penshurst Place in the mid-fourteenth century, he ate beneath a canopy of state, surrounded by his entire household and attended by servants who waited on him on bended knee. His hands were ceremonially washed and dried by two servants before and after the meal. His carver took slices from all the food at his table and tasted them, a precaution against poisoning. His cupbearer served him with drink – again, on bended knee – and held a second cup under his chin to catch the drips. De Pulteney's nineteenth-century counterparts, the fifth Duke of Rutland at Belvoir or the fifteenth Duke of Norfolk at Arundel, would have been horrified at the idea of such formalized ritual. They would also have been appalled at the thought of eating dinner with the servants.

Every attempt to define the country house, to find

a common denominator linking medieval Penshurst with late-Georgian Belvoir while drawing from Restoration Ashdown and a Palladian house of parade like Wanstead, seems doomed to failure. Agriculture, the country house as the headquarters of a working estate, might seem a good candidate, until we turn to the later nineteenth and early twentieth centuries, when plummeting land values meant that agricultural estates lost much of their economic appeal and country house owners sold off land or devoted it to shooting while scrambling for directorships in London's Square Mile as a means of generating desperately needed income. At first glance the social status of the owner also seems promising, one has always had to be relatively rich to build and maintain a country house, and it certainly narrows down the field. But if that is a necessary condition, it is not a sufficient one: any definition lumping together a minor gentry family like the Packers of Groombridge Place with such an immensely powerful nobleman as the first Duke of Devonshire at Chatsworth and failing to account for the wealthy and status-conscious Edwardian industrialist who was quite happy to live in town and not to buy or build a country house, needs careful qualification.

The truth is that there is no common denominator, apart from those which are so general as to be useless: the buildings in this book are all houses, and they all stand or stood in rural settings.

That isn't to say that there is no such thing as the English country house. The mistake lies in thinking that if things are to justify the use of a label, there

must be a quality or set of qualities that is common to all. If we are to understand what connects Penshurst and Groombridge and Belvoir and the rest, the answer perhaps lies not with aesthetics or romantic sentiment, not even with social history or architectural theory; it lies in the arcane world of linguistic philosophy, of all things. Ludwig Wittgenstein in the 1940s was the first to point to concepts that seem to have nothing in common but a label but that rely for their meaning on what he calls family resemblances. 'If you look at them you will

Hampton Court — its immediate surroundings are the most noticeable change.

not see something that is common to all, but similarities, relationships, and a whole series of them at that . . . And the result of this examination is: we see a complicated network of similarities overlapping and criss-crossing: sometimes overall similarities, sometimes similarities of detail.' The concept of the country house is just such a complicated network of relationships. History, art, sociology, politics, economics and architecture – even Vita Sackville-West's patriotic emotionalism – all shed their lights on the stately mansions and

Wollaton's gardens are as beautiful as ever.

manor houses of England. They all present different answers to the question of what a country house is, but none of them in itself provides a complete answer. We take what we want from each discipline and set of attitudes, depending on our interests, our background, our mood at the time, and with those

components we build our own country house.

✤ ✤ ✤

The historical images that serve as a counterpoint to Jason Hawkes' photographs range in time from the medieval cartulary roll depicting Boarstall to C. E. Kempe's late-Victorian line-and-wash drawing of Groombridge Place and the early-twentieth-century views of Ightham Mote and Arundel. The majority, however, date from a period twenty years or so to either side of 1700 – to what is arguably the great age of the country house artist.

In the 1680s Henry Winstanley, who with his views of Audley End in 1678 had published one of the first sets of country house engravings to appear in this country, was advertising his services to 'All Noble men and Gentlemen that please to have their Mansion Houses design'd on Copper Plates' for five or ten pounds and offering 'any Prospect of your house, or any distance, Painted in Oyle of any size att A reasonable rate by me likewise'. Winstanley's other claim to fame was as designer of the first Eddystone Lighthouse, which caused his death when it collapsed in November 1703 – 'the House being his Tomb the Sea his Grave', as the inscription added to his own print of the building recorded. Other artists latched on to the desire of country house builders to publicize their achievements and to distribute likenesses of their new houses and gardens among their friends and neighbours. By the early eighteenth century a number of topographical artists and engravers were specializing in artificially projected aerial perspectives – bird's-eye views – which perfectly displayed the architectural landscapes of the Baroque in all their glory.

The acknowledged masters of the craft and the two men whose names have become synonymous with the bird's-eye view of the country house are Leonard Knyff and Johannes Kip. Their eighty views of country houses, *Britannia Illustrata*, was published in 1707, and their works comprise the lion's share of the prints included here. We owe to them, more than any other artists, a panorama of the English country house during the reigns of William, Anne and George I, which is all the more important because the scenes they depict – many of the houses and all of the gardens – have long since disappeared.

Traditionally Knyff has been thought of as the artist and Kip as the engraver, largely because those are the lines of demarcation followed in *Britannia Illustrata*. In fact, Kip was a considerable topographical artist in his own right: his 1690 bird's-eye of Chelsea Hospital predates by seven years Knyff's earliest recorded view, of Dunham Massey in Cheshire, and the houses that he drew and engraved for Sir Robert Atkyns's *Ancient and Present State of Glostershire* (1712) stand side by side with Knyff's work.

Knyff seems to have begun by working on individual commissions, rather as Winstanley proposed to do in the 1680s. In January 1698 he made an agreement with the Duke of Newcastle 'for drawing engraving & printing three Seats of the said Dukes' – Bolsover Castle, Nottingham Castle and Haughton – and to deliver four hundred prints 'as the

Chatsworth's imposing façades reveal the ambition that built them.

sd Duke shall chuse' for twenty pounds. Advertisements placed by Knyff in May and June 1701 show that he had embarked on a project to draw, engrave and sell by private subscription '100 Noblemens and Gentlemens seats', and that sixty had been completed. Interested subscribers were asked to visit his house at the corner of Old Palace Yard. This scheme was presumably the foundation of the *Britannia Illustrata*, although it was no doubt intended as a collection of prints rather than as a book. By the time that the bookseller David Mortier published the

Britannia six years later Knyff had probably sold his interest in the project.

No working drawings for the engravings have survived, and one would dearly like to know more about how Knyff and Kip operated. Presumably, detailed plans, surveys and elevations were made on site and painstakingly worked up to create the finished prospects. That the two men made personal site visits is suggested by surviving documents. In 1699 the widowed Duchess of Beaufort wrote from Badminton, 'I have had Mr Kniff here, who is doing three drafts . . . my designs when these are all done is to have some of them bound in books & given them to show what a noble place my deare Lord has left.' Much more telling is the evidence provided by the finished views themselves. It used to be said that such aerial perpectives were unreliable, and that because much of their work is undated and is more or less

Now bisected by a busy road, the estate of Leybourne Castle is a thing of the past.

contemporary with new houses and garden layouts, Kip and Knyff were depicting might-have-beens and aspirations rather than recording what they saw. We know this to be true in one or two instances. A 1707 engraving of Wimpole Hall, for example, portrays a projected remodelling that didn't take place, with the original mid-seventeenth-century hall refaced and extended by two bays on either side. In the vast majority of cases where other evidence has survived, however, it corroborates the engravings in every detail – as at Newby Hall in Yorkshire, where in 1697 Celia Fiennes described everything in the Knyff view – from the railings in front of the house to the drying frames behind it – and at Dyrham Park, where the recent discovery of Stephen Switzer's 1718 account confirms the existence of virtually every feature shown in the perspective that Kip had published six years earlier.

The vogue for depicting country houses from the air was a relatively short-lived phenomenon, and after Harris's *Kent* was published in 1719, with views drawn by Thomas Badeslade and engraved by Kip, fashions began to move towards what seem to us today to be the more conventional forms of landscape painting. The popularity of the bird's-eye perspective can perhaps be accounted for by the way in which it was admirably suited to record the Baroque house and garden – which gain so much from a high viewpoint – and by the simple fact of the building boom during the late seventeenth and early eighteenth centuries. 'All the world are running mad after building, as far as they can reach', noted John Vanbrugh in 1708, a

Picture-perfect and timelessly idyllic: Groombridge Place

fact confirmed by Daniel Defoe two decades later. 'Even while the sheets are in the press', he wrote in 1724 in the preface to his *Tour through England and Wales*, 'new beauties appear in several places, and almost to every part we are oblig'd to add appendixes, and supplemental accounts of fine houses, new undertakings, buildings, &c and thus posterity will be continually adding; every age will find an encrease of glory.'

✢ ✢ ✢

Every age has indeed found 'an encrease of glory'. This survey of past and present country houses seen from the air has its fair share of casualties – houses come and go, and that's as it should be – but a

surprising number remain intact from the time when they were engraved, or if they have changed, the change has not diminished them. We still have Knole and Penshurst and Ightham Mote, Elizabethan splendours like Longleat and Wollaton, Caroline gems like Groombridge and Broome and Ashdown.

On a personal note, my own architectural preference is for the Baroque that Kip and Knyff recorded so brilliantly, with all its rhetoric and overblown theatricality. I admire the spirit and drive, even the arrogance and hauteur, of Chatsworth and Castle Howard and Blenheim. But, as anyone can also read in the following pages, I feel a certain ambivalence not only towards the Baroque but towards the very idea of the country house. I don't mourn for the social structures that created it; on the contrary, I exult in their downfall. But I'm still hopelessly in love with their creation.

In an age that has turned the country house into a political football, the reactionary right eulogizes life in the country house as the epitome of gracious living (in their dreams, always the master and mistress, never the second footman or the laundry maid). The liberal left sneers at the heritage industry and castigates us for wallowing in nostalgia and never looking forward to the future. I stand, confused and slightly ashamed, in a morass of ideological and aesthetic ambiguities, angered by both the undemocratic escapism of the right and the shortsightedness of the left – but still infatuated with the startling, breathtaking, extraordinary beauty of the English country house.

CHAPTER ONE

LORDS OF CREATION

❖

*THE COUNTRY HOUSE AS
A STATEMENT OF
POWER AND PRESTIGE*

From the Elizabethan courtier who 'lifted up his lofty towers . . . /That they began to threat the neighbour sky' to the Edwardian brewers and bankers who staked their claim to membership of the Upper Ten Thousand by buying – or building – a castle or a moated manor house, men have seen the country house as more than just a home, more than the administrative headquarters of a great estate. It has been a symbol of belonging, a symbol of ancient lineage – both real and imagined – and, above all, a symbol of wealth and political power.

The Tudors were perhaps the first to understand the potential of architecture as a badge of status. The merchants and entrepreneurs who rose to power during the mid-sixteenth century, men whose social position was tenuous enough for them to need reassurance, were quick to see that a great house was an effective means of confirming and advertising their success to the world.

At the same time, traditional medieval ideas of good lordship were dying away. Even by the late Middle Ages, the lord had rejected the communal lifestyle of his ancestors. Instead of dining in the hall with the rest of the household, seated beneath a canopy of state, served with obeisance and surrounded by ritual and ceremony, he preferred to eat separately in his great chamber. No longer an integral part (even if the most important part) of a small community, he began a process of withdrawal from his servants, which enhanced his power and mystique. Along with these changes passed other old notions that stressed that a nobleman gained re-

A late-eighteenth-century painting of Audley End by William Tompkins.

spect through protecting dependants, offering hospital-
ity to all comers and maintaining a communal lifestyle
with his servants (whom he would refer to, revealingly,
as his 'family'). By Tudor times, the lord's status came
not from what he did but from what he had. His house
and its contents were more potent social indicators
than his behaviour to-
wards his social inferiors,
while their behaviour to-
wards him was condi-
tioned by his wealth and
power rather than by age-
old ties of loyalty.

One result of these
changes was a wave of
spectacular houses – such
as Longleat, Wollaton, Burghley and Audley End – that
sprang up across the country between 1550 and 1630.
With their rooflines overflowing with strapwork cresting and turrets and tall chimneys, their walls vast expanses of glass, these palaces were intended to provoke
not only respect but awe and wonder in all who saw
them. And they did. The odd disapproving voice (like

THE LESSON THAT THE
COUNTRY HOUSE IS A TANGIBLE
EMBODIMENT OF IDEALS AND
ASPIRATIONS — THAT IT HAS
PROPAGANDA VALUE, IN OTHER
WORDS — HAS NEVER
BEEN FORGOTTEN.

that of Ben Jonson, who labelled such houses 'proud,
ambitious heaps') was drowned in the general chorus
of approval. 'So magnificent and stately as the basest
house of a baron doth often match in our days with
some honours of princes in old time', wrote one com-
mentator; 'If ever curious building did flourish in
England, it is in these
our years.'

Once established, the
triumph of form over
function took firm hold,
and it was widely ac-
knowledged that, as Christopher Wren pointed out
in the 1660s, 'Architec-
ture has its political use'.
By the end of the seventeenth century, when many of
the houses in this book were at their peak, this had become a primary motive in the design and decoration of
country houses. More than any other period in English
building, the Baroque was about the ostentatious display of wealth and power.

That display showed itself in the opulence of interior

decoration – the spectacular trompe-l'oeil murals of Verrio and Laguerre and Thornhill, with their soaring and tumbling gods and goddesses ('all without Garments,' noted Celia Fiennes disapprovingly), and the elaborately carved panelling and overmantels of Grinling Gibbons and Edward Pierce, festooned with game and fruit. It showed itself in the typical house plan, in which hall and great chamber were centrally placed on the short axis, with apartments of state – rarely used for everyday living – stretched out stiffly to either side. And it showed itself in the formal gardens that extended internal vistas into the landscape. The spreading wings and great axial avenues of a Blenheim or a Badminton had one function: to impress upon the observer the absolute power of their owner, who could sit in state in his great chamber, presiding over a household of which he was ruler, looking out on a world that his money had tamed and marshalled

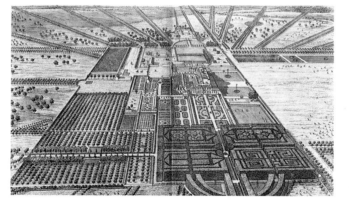

into the straight lines of avenues, canals and parterres.

Inevitably, a reaction to the awesome arrogance of the Baroque set in during the early eighteenth century, as the absolutist ideology that it so perfectly expressed was itself rejected by the Whigs who came to power with George I. By the 1720s Daniel Defoe might still be praising houses like Chatsworth because their magnificence 'express[es] the . . . opulence of the possessor'. His contemporaries at the leading edge of architecture were not so impressed. They were more likely to agree with Colen Campbell's assessment: 'parts . . . without proportion . . .excessive ornaments without grace, and the whole without symmetry'.

''Tis Use alone that sanctifies Expense', wrote Alexander Pope in the early eighteenth century, 'And splendour borrows all her rays from sense.' The truth was that far from being champions of Reason

The early-eighteenth-century aerial perspective of Badminton reveals a world of difference from today's setting.

and Wisdom, engaged in a battle against the profligacies of the past, the new arbiters of taste had merely exchanged one set of values for another. The Palladianism that dominated English country-house architecture during the mid-eighteenth century was in its way just as ideologically motivated as the Baroque.

Take, for example, Campbell's Wanstead in Essex. Built between 1713 and 1720 for an East India magnate, Sir Richard Child, Wanstead consisted of a three-storey block flanked by long two-storey wings. Along the whole façade, symmetry, grace and proportion were the keynotes, and there was hardly any extraneous ornament and none of the dramatic sculptural qualities of a Blenheim or a Castle Howard. A rusticated ground floor (derived from Inigo Jones and Palladio) provided a platform for the piano nobile and accentuated the static, horizontal quality of the design, and a magnificent hexastyle por-

WITH THEIR ROOFLINES OVERFLOWING WITH CRESTING AND TURRETS AND TALL CHIMNEYS, THEIR WALLS VAST EXPANSES OF GLASS, THESE PALACES WERE INTENDED TO PROVOKE NOT ONLY RESPECT BUT AWE AND WONDER IN ALL WHO SAW THEM.

tico gave the building a temple-like quality and at once proclaimed its loyalty to Rome.

Wanstead was one of the most admired and influential houses of its day, giving rise to a host of imitators. Its demolition, a century after it had been completed, was a tragedy. It was also one of the first blows in an essentially ideological battle to leave behind the autocracies of the Stuarts. Rather than emphasizing individual power, it sought to establish its promoters' links with classical civilization, fostering the idea that they were forging a new society to rival that of ancient Rome – a message made clear in the architectural publications of the period, such as Leoni's 1716 translation of Andrea Palladio's *Four Books of Architecture*, in the frontispiece to which Further Time unveils a bust of Palladio while Britannia looks on.

The lesson that the country house is a tangible embodiment of ideals and aspirations – that it has propaganda value, in other words – has never been forgotten. The Georgian gentleman went to Adam for his neo-classical palace, eager to display his culture and civilization to the world. The earnest Victorian nobleman knew that his Gothic Revival mansion conjured up appropriately respectable images of nationhood and God (Gothic was after all more English and more Christian than classical). The Edwardian industrialist used the money earned from his factories to build himself a half-timbered Arts and Crafts

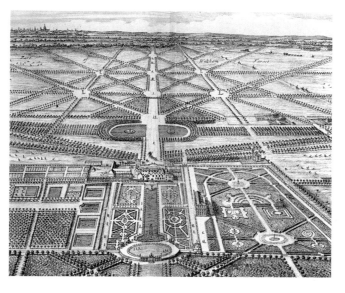

manor house that evoked a cleaner, purer, pre-industrial paradise.

When the fifteenth Duke of Norfolk commissioned C. A. Buckler to create a new castle at Arundel from the ruins of the old one in 1875, his choice of style must surely have been related to a desire to celebrate his family's ancient links with the site, just

as thirty-five years later the wealthy tea importer Julius Drewe built Castle Drogo on the spot in Devon where he had been told his medieval ancestors once lived. ('I wish he didn't want a castle,' wrote his architect Edwin Lutyens, 'but just a delicious lovable house with plenty of good large rooms in it.')

Aspiration and a need to have one's status recognized have always played an important part in the construction of a country house. Whether an Elizabethan entrepreneur legitimizing his new-found wealth, a Jacobean earl building a palace fit for a king, or a Caroline squire keeping up with the latest fashion, the landed classes have used their homes as instruments of prestige. The style might change, the motives might change, but the message was in the medium: for the lords of creation, the country house was more than just a place to live. It was a statement.

BLENHEIM PALACE
Oxfordshire

The Duke of Marlborough, for whom John Vanbrugh designed Blenheim Palace, died in 1722, with the great house still incomplete. He was hardly cold in his grave before the backlash against the Baroque began.

Shaftesbury condemned the palace as 'a false and counterfeit piece of magnificence'. Pope mocked its grandeur. Horace Walpole loathed it, characterizing it as 'execrable within, without, & almost all round'. And on visiting days polite Georgian society flocked to sneer at the discredited Vanbrugh.

It took a fellow artist to appreciate the scale of Vanbrugh's achievement. Speaking to the Royal Academy in 1786, Joshua Reynolds told his students, 'In the buildings of Vanbrugh, who was a poet as well as an architect, there is a greater display of imagination than we shall find perhaps in any other.' A few years later Richard Payne Knight took up Reynolds's cue:

It appears to me that at Blenheim, Vanbrugh conceived and executed a very bold and difficult design . . . and that in spite of the many faults with which he is very justly reproached, he has formed, in a style truly his own, a well-combined whole, a mansion worthy of a great prince and warrior.

This is, of course, the key to our understanding of Blenheim. The palace was intended from the first to be 'a

A 1752 engraving by
Boydell, showing
Vanbrugh's Grand Bridge
to the right.

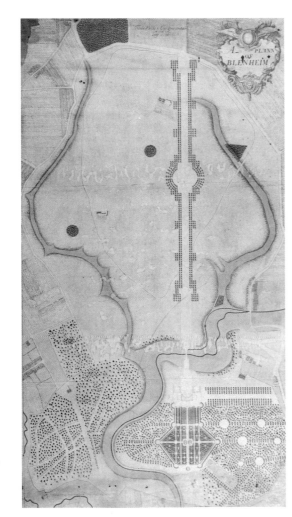

An early-eighteenth-
century garden plan. The
walks and bastions at the
bottom of the picture are
derived from plans of
fortifications designed for
Louis XIV.

❖

'POSTERITY WHEN THEY VIEW IN
THIS HOUSE THE TROPHIES OF THE
DUKE OF MARLBOROUGH'S FAME,
AND THE GLORIES OF HIS GREAT
ACHIEVEMENTS WILL NOT CELEBRATE
HIS NAME ONLY;
BUT WILL LOOK ON BLENHEIM
HOUSE AS A MONUMENT OF
THE GENEROUS TEMPER OF THE
ENGLISH NATION.'
Daniel Defoe, A Tour Through England and
Wales (1726)

❖

mansion worthy of a great prince and warrior', a monument to Marlborough's victory at the little Danube village that gave it its name.

It remains a monument. The formality of the seven acres of buildings and courts are augmented rather than softened by Capability Brown's changes to the surrounding landscape. The fantastical skyline and receding planes of the fortress-like entrance façade are just as dramatic as they were when they were created. Blenheim is indeed a monument, not just to the Duke of Marlborough but to the genius of John Vanbrugh.

The entrance façade, just as dramatic as when it was first created nearly three centuries ago.

ALTHORP
Northamptonshire

John Evelyn made several visits to Althorp, then the seat of Robert Spencer, Earl of Sunderland. His diary entry for 14 July 1675 notes that it was 'placed in a pretty open bottome, very finely watred and flanqued with stately woods'. The house itself was 'a kind of modern building of freestone', although the kitchen and chapel were too small, and there were some mean outbuildings spoiling the scene.

By the time of his next stay, in August 1688, Evelyn's praise was considerably more lavish. The 'roomes of state, gallerys, offices and furniture [were] such as may become a great Prince', the garden was 'exquisitely planted and kept'. The Countess was 'wise and noble', the servants were neat and clean, and everything – from the service at table to the general air of order and decency – was worthy of comment. The only sour notes were caused by the absent Earl, who had professed his conversion to Catholicism when James II came to the throne, much to Evelyn's disapproval; and his eldest son, Lord Spencer, about whom one would like to know more. 'Rambling about the world, [he] dishonours both his name and his family, adding sorrow to sorrow to a mother who has taken all imaginable care of his education'.

In the thirteen years between Evelyn's two visits, the Earl of Sunderland completed a sweeping modernization (begun, in fact, as early as 1666) of his old home, which had been in the family since 1508. The interiors were remodelled, the two gable-ended wings of the Tudor building were given

'Roomes of state . . . such as may become a greate Prince': Althorp in the early eighteenth century (Kip and Knyff).

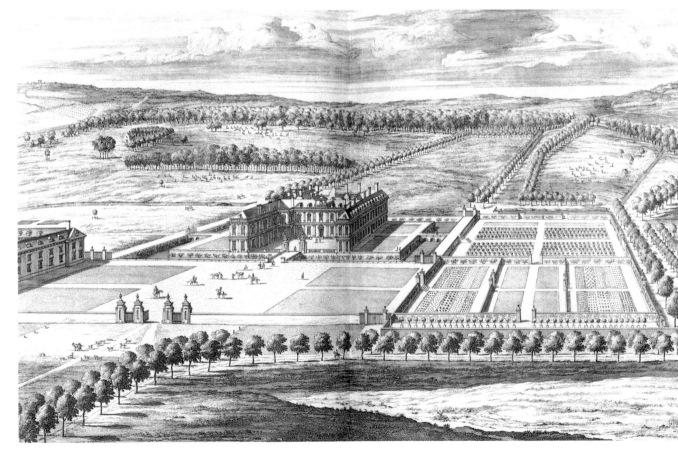

hipped roofs and dormers, the first-floor windows were given segmental pediments, and the small court behind the entrance façade was roofed over to form a top-lit staircase hall.

Althorp's illustrious architectural history, however, was far from over. Between 1729 and 1733 Roger Morris remodelled the interiors once more and replaced the stables with a beautiful Palladian quadrangle, with towers at the four corners that derive from Inigo Jones's south front of Wilton. And between 1787 and 1791 Henry Holland introduced the only regrettable feature in an otherwise perfect building. We

can forgive him the classical pediment to the centre of the entrance front, even the fact that he filled in the Tudor moat. Much harder to forgive are the drab, grey tiles that cover up the red brick and stone dressings of the earlier house.

The surprisingly simple garden layout shown in Knyff's view has given way to a formal garden by W. M. Teulon, laid out between 1860 and 1863. Teulon was also responsible for the present stone pillars and ironwork to the forecourt. The dining room, which projects to the east, was added by MacVicar Anderson in about 1877.

Althorp today: the Palladian stable block to the left (1729-33) is the work of Roger Morris.

The King's Gallery, put up in 1695, is still the dominant feature of the south front.

KENSINGTON PALACE
London

'Kensington, where for aire our great King William bought a house and fitted it for a retirement with pretty gardens' – so Celia Fiennes summed up in 1701 the great palace that William III had begun to create in what was then a country village, a couple of miles west of Whitehall and the City.

The house had been built in 1605 for Sir George Coppin, James I's Clerk to the Crown. It was later sold to Sir Heneage Finch, whose son was created Earl of Nottingham in 1681. When William and Mary were seeking a convenient residence close to London – Hampton Court was too far away for daily use, while the polluted air and damp fogs that hung over Whitehall aggravated the King's asthma – they finally decided on Nottingham House, as it was then known, and purchased the estate in 1689 for 18,000 guineas.

In July of that year Christopher Wren enlarged the Jacobean house with the help of Nicholas Hawksmoor: four pavilions were added to the corners of the original building, there were separate apartments for the King and Queen, and two great galleries were created. The Queen's Gallery, which runs north from the north-west pavilion, dates from 1690-1. The severe but imposing King's Gallery was put up in 1695, after Mary's death the previous year had caused William to abandon plans for rebuilding Hampton Court.

The palace remained a favourite with William's successors, even if each modified the building and its grounds in his or her own way. Anne swept away her brother-in-law's Dutch gardens and built the Orangery to the north. George I demolished Coppin's original house and replaced it with three new state rooms decorated by William Kent. George II and Caroline of Anspach landscaped the grounds again, using plans that Henry Wise had drawn up in Anne's reign – the Round Pond dates from 1728 and the Serpentine from 1730.

Kensington Palace in the early eighteenth century. The asthmatic William of Orange bought the house in 1689 as a retreat from the polluted air and damp fogs of Whitehall.

❖

'THE HOUSE IT-SELF FRONTS TO THE GARDEN THREE WAYS, THE GARDENS BEING NOW MADE EXCEEDING FINE, AND ENLARGED TO SUCH A DEGREE, AS TO REACH QUITE FROM THE GREAT ROAD TO KENSINGTON TOWN, TO THE ACTON ROAD NORTH, MORE THAN A MILE.'
Daniel Defoe, *A Tour Through England and Wales* (1726)

❖

A U D L E Y   E N D
Essex

'Too large for a King, though it might do for a Lord Treasurer.' James I's caustic pronouncement brings home to us the awesome impression of grandeur and magnificence that Audley End once presented, an impression that it is easy to forget, now that much of the house has been demolished.

The Lord Treasurer in question was Thomas Howard, Earl of Suffolk, who began building Audley End in 1603. The best evidence we have of its original appearance is a view by Henry Winstanley published in 1678, nine years after the house had been sold to Charles II. It shows the building grouped around two courtyards in a series of dramatic receding planes, like stage scenery. The entrance, marked by four circular turrets and flanked by two towers, gave onto the western court, in which the principal apartments were on the north and south, over open piazzas. The great hall stood opposite the entrance, with porches at either end and a central oriel to emphasize its importance. The inner court contained further state lodgings and a long gallery aligned with hall and gatehouse to the east.

Howard's architect is not known, although Vertue suggests that the surveyor was Bernard Janssen, who also worked on Northumberland House (1605-9) for Howard's uncle, the first Earl of Northampton.

The Lord Treasurer's career in public office suggests that King James's remarks were more than a casual aside. It was common knowledge that Howard's wife was extorting money from those who had business at the Treasury in return

Audley End in all its glory: Henry Winstanley's 1678 view, from a set of engravings entitled Ground Platts, General and Particular Prospects of all the Parts of His Majesty's Royal Pallace of Audley End.

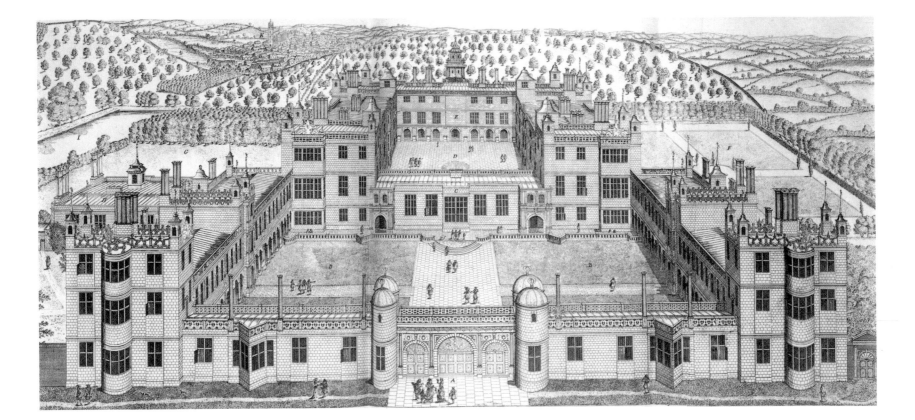

A late-eighteenth-century view, from the south-west, by William Tompkins.

for using her influence with her husband, and in 1618, two years after Audley End was completed, Howard was himself charged with embezzlement, committed to the Tower and fined £30,000. We shall never know how much public money was diverted to the building of his great house, but as a statement of power and prestige it has seldom been surpassed.

It scarcely lasted a hundred years. Charles II didn't stump up the cash for his purchase, and William III returned Audley End to the Howard family in 1701. By this time their fortunes were in decline, and they couldn't maintain the building. In 1721 the eighth Earl of Suffolk demolished the western court, leaving the inner court intact. Thirty years later the eastern range was also razed, leaving only the hall and two wings.

Although only the hall range and two wings survive today, Audley End is still an imposing house.

❖

'THE HOUSE AT AUDLEY END WAS IN FORMER TIMES THE LARGEST PLACE IN ALL ENGLAND, AND, ALTHOUGH A GREAT PART OF IT HAS BEEN PULLED DOWN, IT REMAINS ONE OF THE MOST PERFECT PIECES OF ARCHITECTURE IN THE KINGDOM.'
Count Frederick Kielmansegge, *Diary of a Journey to England* (1762)

❖

RAGLEY HALL
Warwickshire

Ragley is one of the few surviving examples of the architecture of Robert Hooke, described by John Aubrey as 'certainly the greatest Mechanick this day in the World'.

A list of the men who shaped the development of English architecture during the late seventeenth century would contain few artisans raised in the building trades. Instead, it would comprise mainly gentlemen amateurs, some of whom went on to make a career in architecture, others who remained content to dabble. Roger Pratt, one of the most influential figures in Caroline country-house design, trained as a lawyer and produced only five houses before retiring to the life of a squire on his Norfolk estate. William Winde was a professional soldier and military engineer. Vanbrugh was a successful playwright and captain of marines. Sir Christopher Wren was a brilliant academic, a mathematician and astronomer.

Robert Hooke, the designer of Ragley Hall, was one of the most gifted members of this set. Although he never made a career of architecture, the geometry professor and curator of experiments to the Royal Society designed a number of buildings, many of which were characterized

by his interest in contemporary French architecture.

Ragley is one of the few surviving examples of Hooke's work as an architect. His client, the first Earl of Conway, had initially consulted a local master carpenter named Hurlbutt, and the earliest parts of the house, the two service blocks flanking the entrance court, were erected in about 1677. Hurlbutt also provided a 'model' for the main block, but Conway clearly wanted something more sophisticated: in 1679 he called in Hooke to modify the design.

Perhaps Conway was influenced by Hooke's recent work for Ralph Montagu at Montagu House in Bloomsbury (1675-9), 'a fine palace built after the French pavilion way', according to Evelyn. Certainly the most notable feature of the design is the four corner pavilions that give Ragley its distinctively French air.

The Earl of Conway died without heirs – and with Ragley's interiors still unfinished – in 1683, and the estate passed to his cousin Popham Conway. Knyff's view was executed shortly before Popham's own death in 1699. The interiors

View by Knyff, c. 1699. The house was still unfinished at this time, and the garden design may never have been executed.

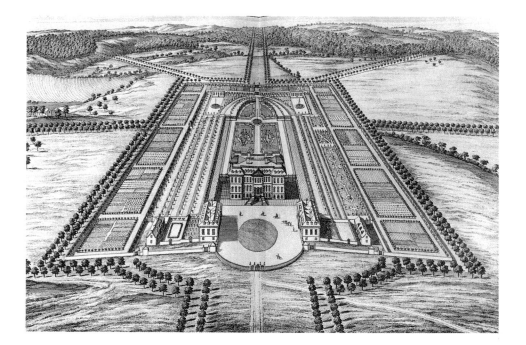

were finished by James Gibbs in the 1750s. The exterior remains much as it was in Hooke's time, save for the Ionic portico added by James Wyatt in the 1780s and the roof balustrade, which was lowered at the same time. Wyatt also demolished the two service blocks and built the stable court. The formal French gardens, if they were ever completed, had already been swept away in 1758 when Capability Brown landscaped the park.

The corner pavilions give Ragley a distinctively French air.

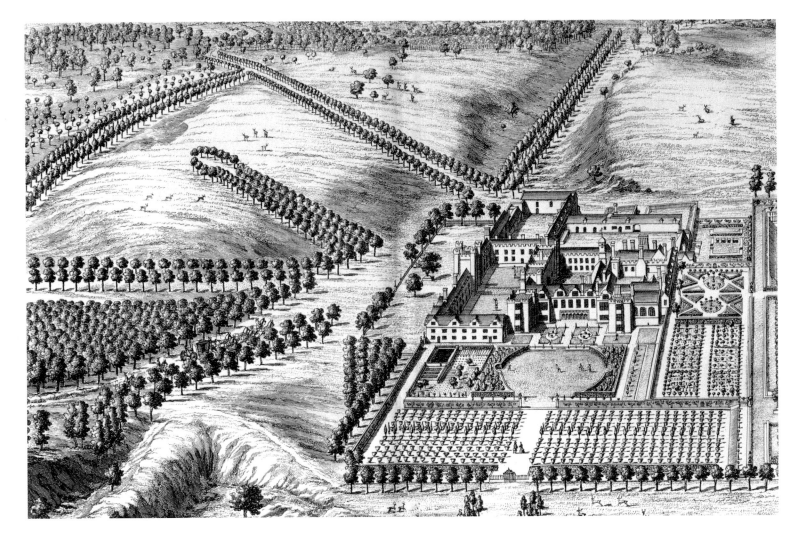

'*I WHO AM
SOMETHING OF A
LOVER OF ALL
ANTIQUITIES MUST
BE A VERY GREAT
ADMIRER OF
KNOLE. I THINK
IT THE MOST
INTERESTING
THING IN
ENGLAND.*'
Edmund Burke, letter to
Duke of Dorset (1791)

*Prospect of Knole from
the south, engraved by
Kip (c. 1707).*

*Enlarged and altered
several times since it was
built in the fifteenth
century, Knole's
sprawling courtyards and
irregular façades still
have a medieval air about
them.*

KNOLE
Kent

Knole dates from the later fifteenth century, when
Thomas Bourchier, Archbishop of Canterbury,
built a substantial house grouped around a series
of courtyards. After Bourchier's death in 1486, it remained an
archiepiscopal palace until 1538, when Henry VIII bullied
Cranmer into presenting it to the Crown. The King enlarged
the house by constructing three new ranges of lodgings and a
turreted and crenellated gatehouse in front of the
Archbishop's original gatehouse, thus forming what is now the
main entrance court. After his death, the house changed

occupants several times in quick succession before Elizabeth I
granted it to Thomas Sackville in June 1566.

Sackville is chiefly remembered today as the co-author
with Thomas Norton of *Gorboduc*, the first tragedy written in
English – and perhaps the dullest. But he also played a
significant role in late-sixteenth-century politics, rising
to become Lord High Treasurer and Lord High Steward
of England. He was just the sort of wealthy courtier
whom one might have expected to make the most of
his new acquisition by building a great house.

36

A late-eighteenth-century pen-and-wash drawing by Hendrick Franz de Cort.

'AT SUNSET I HAVE SEEN THE SILHOUETTE OF THE GREAT BUILDING STAND DEAD BLACK ON A RED SKY; ON MOONLIGHT NIGHTS IT STANDS BLACK AND SILENT, WITH GLINTING WINDOWS, LIKE AN ENCHANTED CASTLE. ON MISTY AUTUMN NIGHTS I HAVE SEEN IT EMERGING PARTIALLY FROM THE TRAILS OF VAPOUR, AND HEARD THE LONELY ROAR OF THE RED DEER ROAMING UNDER THE WALLS.'

Vita Sackville-West, *Knole and the Sackvilles* (1922)

John Harris's 1720 engraving of Knole from the west.

And so he might, if he had had the chance. But Knole was tenanted when Elizabeth gave it to him, the result of a complicated series of lettings and sublettings in the 1550s and early 1560s. For thirty-seven years he was unable even to live there, much less to replace it with something more in keeping with the latest architectural fashions. When he did finally gain possession in 1603, he was in his late sixties: Elizabeth was dead, and he may have felt that the uncertainties of old age and a new reign made it an unpropitious time to build. Or perhaps he felt with Francis Bacon that 'it is a reverend thing to see an ancient castle or building not in decay'.

However, his reverence for the venerable structure didn't deter him from turning it into the sort of place that was appropriate for someone of his standing. The interiors were remodelled, and the exterior was brought up to date by adding distinctively Jacobean shaped gables, decorated with obelisks and topped with leopards (the Sackville family crest).

Because Sackville was reluctant to do away with the old house entirely, Knole has little of the symmetry of its contemporaries. Ironically, it is the very sense of organic, centuries-long development so little valued by Sackville's peers that led them to sweep away the past that to our eyes makes the house one of the most attractive in England.

One of the most attractive houses in England.

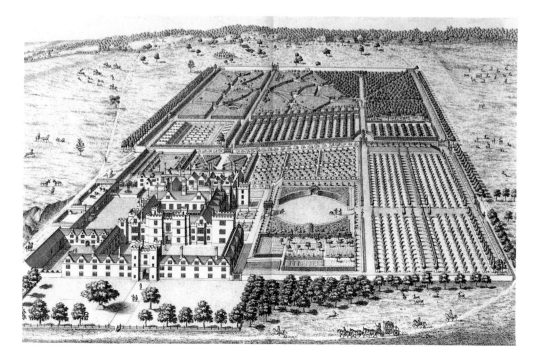

The courtyard, looking up at the medieval shell keep (James Canter, c. 1778).

ARUNDEL
Sussex

William Daniell's 1823 view across the River Arun.

The owners of Arundel Castle have played a pivotal role in British social and political life since 1067, when Roger de Montgomery was created Earl of Arundel (and granted a third of Sussex) for his stewardship of Normandy while William was away conquering England. The Fitzalans, who acquired the castle in 1243, fought at Crecy and Beauvais; a Fitzalan carried the crown at the coronation of Richard II.

The family tree of the Howards, Earls of Arundel and Dukes of Norfolk, who inherited the castle through marriage to a Fitzalan heiress in 1555, is even more illustrious. The third Duke managed to marry off two of his nieces — Anne Boleyn and Katherine Howard — to Henry VIII; the fourth tried to marry Mary Queen of Scots and lost his head — and the dukedom — on Tower Hill in 1572. Philip Howard, who died in the Tower for having a Mass said for the victory of the Spanish Armada, was canonized. And the sixteenth Duke of Norfolk (the title was restored in 1660) was manager of the England cricket team in 1962-3.

Arundel has had an equally chequered history. The basic medieval layout survives — a twelfth-century shell keep perched on top of de Montgomery's high motte, with baileys to the north and east. But the castle was sacked and left in ruins during the Civil War, and sporadic attempts to

restore it in the eighteenth and nineteenth centuries culminated in a massive rebuilding programme, carried out by C. A. Buckler for the fifteenth Duke of Norfolk between about 1875 and 1900.

Arundel thus essentially belongs not to the Middle Ages but to a tradition of mock medievalism that includes Belvoir in Leicestershire (James Wyatt, 1800-25), Wyattville's work at Windsor (1824-40), the Norman Revival castle that

Thomas Hopper designed at Penrhyn (1825-44) and, of course, William Burges's wonderfully flamboyant reconstruction of Cardiff Castle between 1868 and 1885.

Limping in at the tail end of this tradition, Buckler's work at Arundel is rather less colourful. In fact, it exhibits a pathological earnestness that must have seemed oddly outmoded even as the rebuilding began.

C. A. Buckler's late-Victorian rebuilding exhibits a pathological earnestness that seems rather ponderous today.

BROOME PARK
Kent

Some seventeenth-century country houses, such as Audley End and Chatsworth, impress us with the power and arrogance of their conception. They are first and foremost ideological declarations, and from our late twentieth-century viewpoint we can sense just by looking at them their owners' frightening presumption and hauteur. Others, like Groombridge Place or Whixley, are more domestic. Their builders, we feel, were creating homes rather than political statements. Their owners were content to be moulded by, rather than to mould, the society they lived in.

Broome Park falls into neither of these categories. Its attraction is purely aesthetic. It is beautiful, and everything else – its owner's social aspirations, his lifestyle, his place in the cultural context of the time – pales into insignificance beside the experience of that beauty.

Broome was built between 1635 and 1638 for Sir Basil Dixwell, a Warwickshire man who inherited land near Folkestone from an uncle and settled in Kent as a result. His

Broome in 1720, engraved by John Harris for Thomas Badeslade's Views of Kent Seats.

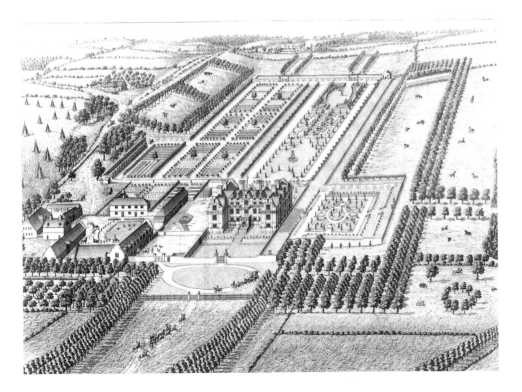

architect, whose name remains a mystery, produced a perfectly symmetrical H-plan house of cut and moulded red brick in the same tradition as Raynham Hall, Norfolk (1635), the Dutch House at Kew (1631) and Swakeleys, Middlesex (1638). Like them, Broome is the product of a concerted campaign by Caroline bricklayers to demonstrate that they could build houses without the help of masons. Also like them, it produced a display of stunning virtuosity. The long pilaster strips and the windows, which until the house was restored in the early twentieth century gradually increased in depth from the ground floor upwards, naturally direct the eye to the astonishing sculptural display that distinguishes the roofline. Scrolls and triangular pediments, broken pediments pushing up to the sky, pediments piled one on top of another – some pierced by windows, others standing free above the roof – the effect is breathtaking, a joy in creation and freedom from restraint that still makes one marvel today.

Broome Park's interiors were remodelled by James Wyatt in 1778, and there were a number of changes (including the altered fenestration) for Lord Kitchener between 1911 and 1916. The brick stables, also with shaped gables, are contemporary with Dixwell's house.

An astonishing sculptural display by Caroline bricklayers.

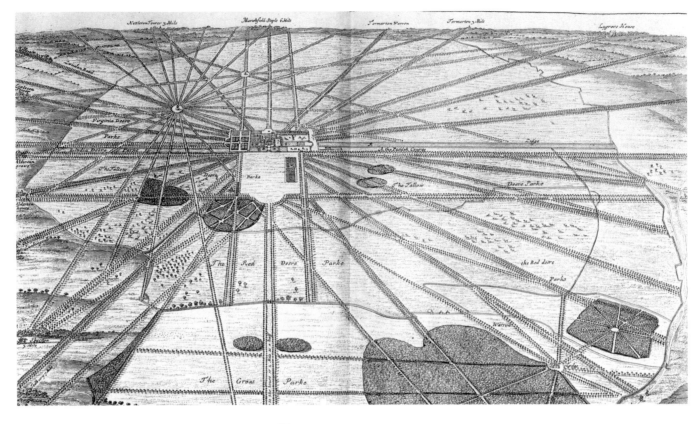

'Divers of the gentlemen
cut their trees and hedges
to humour [the Duke of
Beaufort's] vistos; and
some planted their hills
in his lines for
compliment at their own
charge.' (View by Knyff
and Kip, c. 1700)

BADMINTON
Avon

Henry, first Duke of Beaufort, wielded his power like a medieval overlord rather than a Stuart courtier. This 'Most Noble & Potent Prince', as Kip's engraving calls him, kept feudal state at Badminton with a household of two hundred. His influence in Gloucestershire was so great that it shaped the landscape far beyond the confines of Badminton itself. According to Roger North, 'divers of the gentlemen cut their trees and hedges to humour his vistos; and some planted their hills in his lines for compliment at their own charge.'

The house at the heart of this huge network of avenues and rides has a complicated history. In 1655 the Duke (then Lord Herbert – he was elevated to the dukedom by Charles II in 1682) inherited the estate from a cousin, at which time there was a Jacobean remodelling of an earlier

house on the site. After the Restoration Herbert embarked on a twenty-seven-year campaign to modernize the building, employing many of the craftsmen who worked with Sir Christopher Wren at the King's Works, including Grinling Gibbons and the master carpenter Matthew Banckes. The architect of the new building is unknown, although it has been suggested that the Duke may have had a hand in its design.

The main façade at Badminton was, and still is, the north front shown in Kip's engraving. After the first Duke's remodelling, the nine-bay main block on this front was dominated by a rather Jonesian five-bay centrepiece of three storeys, with two bays to either side. The slightly projecting lower storey was rusticated, and the upper two were given a giant colonnade with Composite capitals. The rest of the block was five storeys high, but by a curiously naïve piece of

*The architect of
Badminton is unknown,
but the Duke of Beaufort
himself may have
contributed to the design.*

planning, their windows were unrelated to those in the centre. The whole was crowned by a balustrade and cupola and flanked by two lower wings ending in hipped-roof pavilions with flat single-storey entrances.

The first Duke of Beaufort died in 1700, and for most of the following century his descendants spent vast sums in bringing Badminton into line with contemporary fashions. The anomalies in the fenestration of the north front were ironed out in the 1730s, when Smith of Warwick replaced the five-storey parts of the façade with three storeys of windows to match the centrepiece. In the 1740s William Kent gave the central five bays a classical pediment, with open cupolas to either side. Kent also helped deformalize the gardens, but the remains of the first Duke's avenues can still be made out.

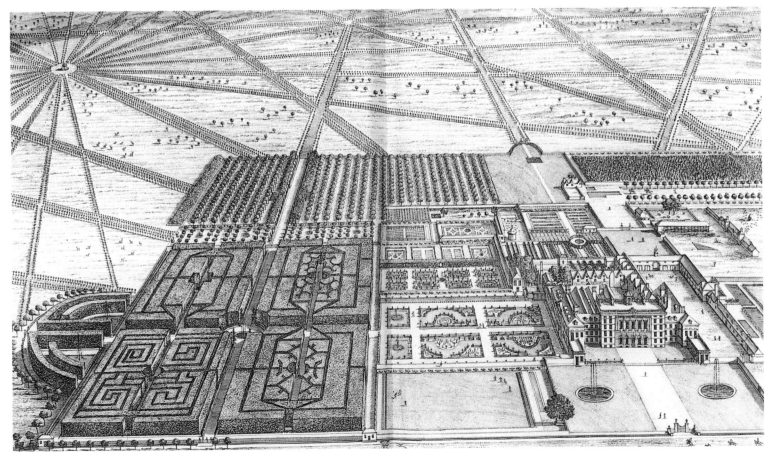

William Kent added the pediment and cupolas in the mid-eighteenth century.

Although the formal landscape has long since vanished, it is still possible to make out the vestiges of Beaufort's great network of avenues and rides.

The original north front, with its Jonesian five-bay centrepiece. (Knyff and Kip, c. 1700)

CHAPTER TWO

NATURE TAMED

❖

GARDENS AND LANDSCAPES —
THE COUNTRY HOUSE
IN ITS SETTING

'The new mode of Gravel Walks and Grass-plots is . . . now become presidents [precedents] for many stately Country Residencies . . . But it's hoped that this new, useless, and unpleasant mode, will like many other vanities grow out of Fashion.' So wrote John Worlidge in 1683, and how right he was in his prediction that gravel walks and grass plots would grow out of fashion. But how wrong-headed he was in his condemnation of the formal country-house garden, which must be one of the great achievements of English landscape design.

If one had to choose the most dramatic visual difference between a country house at the beginning of the eighteenth century — the point at which it is captured so vividly by many of the engravings in this book — and that same country house today, architectural change would take second place to the radical modifications made to the surrounding landscape over the last three hundred years. Hardly anything remains of the canals and fountains, the symmetrical compartments divided by balustrades and carefully clipped hedges, the avenues and vistas. With a few exceptions they have been supplanted by the bland mediocrity of the landscape park, with all of its clumps and belts of trees and irregular, artificial bodies of water. Nature tamed has been replaced by Nature maimed.

Too harsh? Of course. Regret at the disappearance of so many magnificent Baroque gardens shouldn't make us see the landscape designers of the later eighteenth century as vandals who wantonly laid waste to works of art, destroying them as carelessly — and as irrevocably —

Melton Constable in Norfolk. By the later seventeenth century, a desire to dominate nature had become a moving force in garden design.

48

as any bulldozer. That is absurd. All periods, all styles, have something to give to us, and that holds as true for the schemes of Capability Brown or Humphry Repton as it does for the gardens they replaced. But so many of the later schemes survive. It seems unfair that the stately formality of their predecessors has gone for ever.

That formality had its roots in the Renaissance and in the Tudor discovery of Renaissance theory. Just as the Elizabethan country house was required to display the Vitruvian properties of harmony, proportion and symmetry, so must the garden that surrounded it conform to the same values. Within well-defined and secure enclosures (made necessary by the need to keep out the cattle, sheep and deer that grazed the parkland), elaborate knot gardens of box, grass, and even brick-dust and white sand, were contained within straight hedges of elm, holly and hawthorn, and embellished with statuary, fountains and

AMONG ENGLISH GARDEN DESIGNERS OF THE LATE SEVENTEENTH CENTURY TWO NAMES STAND OUT: GEORGE LONDON AND HENRY WISE. AFTER 1687 THEY LAID OUT MANY OF THE MOST IMPORTANT TURN-OF-THE-CENTURY GARDENS.

topiary. The more artificial the result, the better. During a visit to Hampton Court in 1599, one German traveller was astonished to see 'men and women, half men and half horse, sirens, serving-maids with baskets, French lilies and delicate crenellations all round made from dry twigs bound together and . . . evergreen quick-set shrubs'. In a rather less approving passage written twelve years earlier, William Harrison remarked, 'So curious and cunning are our gardeners now in these days that they presume to do in manner what they list with Nature, and moderate her course in things as if they were her superiors.'

By the later seventeenth century a desire to express dominion over nature had become a moving force in garden design, just as it was in the creation of country houses. The inspiration for both came from the Low Countries, where numbers of Royalists had spent their exile during the Commonwealth, and from France,

The entrance front, church and stables of Wimpole Hall, Cambridgeshire.

where Le Nôtre's work at Versailles would influence the layout of English noblemen's gardens for a generation. Le Nôtre's reputation was such that within weeks of being restored to the throne in 1660, and even before the French Royal Gardener had begun work at Versailles, Charles II asked his cousin Louis XIV

field's Bretby Park, where the grounds were once described as the finest in Europe outside Versailles. Celia Fiennes visited Bretby in 1698 and marvelled at the canals and fountains, in particular at 'a Clock which by the water worke is moved and strikes the hours and chimes the quarters, and when they

if he could borrow him to work on the grounds of Greenwich Palace.

Another Frenchman, Monsieur Grillet, a pupil of Le Nôtre's, laid out the cascade and other waterworks at Chatsworth in the 1690s. Grillet was also responsible for the waterworks at one of the most celebrated gardens in England – the Earl of Chester-

please play[s] Lilibolaro on the Chymes'.

Among English garden designers of the period, two names stand out from the rest: George London and Henry Wise. London, who had founded a nursery in Chelsea in 1681, went into partnership with Wise six years later, and together they laid out many of the most important turn-of-the-century gardens. As Royal Gardeners to Queen Anne, they worked at Windsor and Hampton Court and Kensington Palace. They designed the gardens that accompanied Grillet's waterworks at Chatsworth. Together or separately they laid out new gardens at Longleat, Newby Hall in Yorkshire and almost certainly at Wimpole in Cambridgeshire, where the Earl of Radnor spent so much money on improvements that he was forced to sell up and move out. They were also responsible for the grand scheme at Blenheim, a huge formal garden with a network of walks and bastions to the south of the palace that was derived, appropriately, from fortifications created for Louis XIV's campaigns, a homage to the Duke of Marlborough's military prowess.

By the time that Blenheim was being laid out in the early eighteenth century, however, the great days of the formal garden were already fading, and Worlidge's disdain for 'this . . . useless, and unpleasant mode' was

THE MAIN REASONS FOR THE FALL OF THE FORMAL GARDEN WERE IDEOLOGICAL — LIKE THE BAROQUE PALACE THAT MIGHT STAND AT ITS HEART, ITS RADIATING AVENUES AND WALKS SMACKED OF ABSOLUTISM — AND AESTHETIC.

coming to be shared by others. The economics of maintaining precision and regularity on such a vast scale were prohibitive; at Canons in Middlesex the turf was scythed two or three times every week and weeded every day. The need to maintain a distinct partition between the artifice of a garden and the more 'natural' landscape of the surrounding parkland was obviated by the introduction of the sunken fence, or ha-ha, which allowed park and garden to form a visually coherent whole while keeping stock away from the house.

But the main reasons for the fall of the formal garden were ideological — like the Baroque palace that might stand at its heart, its radiating avenues and walks smacked to the early Georgians of absolutism and the bad old tyrannies of the Stuarts — and aesthetic. In 1712 Joseph Addison published an essay in the *Spectator*, in which he argued that 'there is something more bold and masterly in the rough careless strokes of Nature, than in the nice touches and embellishments of Art'. For Addison there was something intrinsically superior about natural objects in which the hand of Man was absent, or at least unobtrusive: 'I would rather look upon a tree in all its luxuriancy and diffusion of boughs and branches, than when it is thus cut and trimmed into a mathematical figure; and cannot but fancy that an orchard in flower looks infinitely more delightful, than all the little labyrinths of the most finished parterre.'

Others took up Addison's call for an end to the formality of the Baroque. Pope heaped scorn on the sort of garden in which

No pleasing Intricacies intervene,

No artful wildness to perplex the scene;

Grove nods at grove, each Alley has a brother,

And half the platform just reflects the other.

The suff'ring eye inverted Nature sees,

Trees cut to Statutes, Statues thick as trees.

Wilton House, Wiltshire. John Evelyn declared that the gardens were 'esteem'd the noblest in England'.

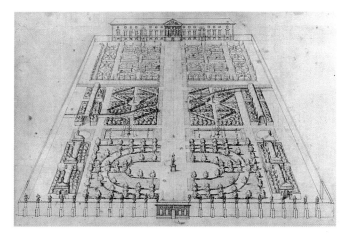

William Kent, in Walpole's famous phrase, 'leaped the fence and saw that all nature was a garden'. Within a decade or two the country house had bade adieu (to quote Walpole again) 'to canals, circular basons and cascades tumbling down marble steps . . . Dealing in none but the colours of nature . . . men saw a new creation opening before their eyes. The living landscape was chastened and polished, not transformed.'

The results are all around us. Everywhere, country house owners rushed to embrace the taste for a more naturalistic – though equally artificial – landscape, a taste that found its greatest exponent in Capability Brown. He transformed the grounds of many of the houses in this book – Althorp and Blenheim, Chatsworth and Longleat, Ragley and Temple Newsam and Wilton and Wrest. One by one, the formal gardens that provided such an exquisitely beautiful setting for those houses were swept away.

NEWBY HALL
North Yorkshire

Because so few late-seventeenth-century garden layouts have survived intact, one often wonders if Knyff's views portray what was actually on the ground. Does the engraving reflect the owner's plans and aspirations rather than the reality? Did he ever parade past the fountains and statues and parterres, or show off his avenues and walks to admiring neighbours?

There are no such doubts where Newby Hall is concerned, because an eye-witness account corroborates every detail. Built to the designs of an unknown architect in the early 1690s, Sir Edward Blackett's house was visited by Celia Fiennes in 1697, five years after London and Wise had supplied trees for the new gardens. Her characteristically enthusiastic description – 'the finest house I saw in Yorkshire' – coincides exactly with Knyff's view. The iron gates are there before the house, 'all painted blew and gold tipps', the main gate 'made large in a compass like a halfe Moone'. The gardens to the right of the house contain 'grass plotts 4 square with 5 brass Statues great and small in each Square', while those to the left are 'full of

dwarfe trees both fruites and green, set cross ways which lookes very finely'. She even confirms that the curious enclosure behind the house and to one side of the double avenue is a drying ground, 'a Landry Close with frames for drying of cloths, wall'd in'.

Although the gardens that Celia admired so much have gone, Edward Blackett's Newby remains, despite being much altered between 1767 and 1785. During that period the virtuoso William Weddell, whose father bought the estate in the mid-century, commissioned Robert Adam to produce a suitable setting for his collection of sculpture and works of art. In addition to remodelling the interiors – some of his best work – Adam designed the columned entrance porch and the two low wings that flank Blackett's original house. He also created the quadrangular stable block that stands near the site of the original stables and coach house shown in Knyff's view.

Every detail of Knyff's 1707 prospect is corroborated by Celia Fiennes's account of Newby, right down to the drying frames behind the house.

The two low wings and the stable block were added by Robert Adam between 1767 and 1785.

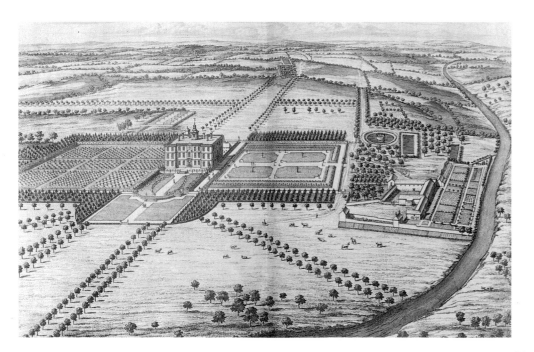

❖

'THERE ARE GOOD STABLES AND COACH-HOUSE AND ALL THE OFFICES ARE VERY CONVENIENT, VERY GOOD CELLARS ALL ARCH'D AND THERE I DRANKE SMALL BEER FOUR YEARS OLD — NOT TOO STALE, VERY CLEAR GOOD BEER WELL BREW'D.'

Celia Fiennes, *My Northern Journey* (1697)

❖

A formal pond in the gardens.

Little remains of Edward Blackett's late-seventeenth-century garden layout.

Newby, with the River Ure in the background.

CHIRK CASTLE
Clwyd

Begun in the late thirteenth century as a response to the rebellion against Anglo-Norman rule that broke out in Wales in 1294, Chirk Castle was intended to be rather more forbidding than it is today. Like the royal castle of Beaumaris, which was built around the same time, it was probably planned as a rectangle almost twice the size of the present building, with drum towers at each corner and a semicircular tower in the centre of each front. Of that early medieval castle, only the three towers on the north front and just over half of the west and east ranges survive, much altered. The rest has vanished – if, indeed, it was ever built.

In spite of repairs made during the fifteenth and early sixteenth centuries, the castle had fallen into ruin by Elizabeth's reign, when a survey reported that 'though yt doth seeme very fayre . . . [it] is utterly ruinous, the Tymber rotten, and wthout hope of well repairinge'.

By the time Badeslade's view was taken in 1735, the Myddleton family, who bought Chirk in 1595, had done more than their fair share of repairing. The old castle had been converted into a house. Half of that house had been pulled down by Lambert, who in 1659 was instructed by Parliament to 'see that Chirke Castle be demolished and made untenable', and rebuilt during the Restoration. The trees in the park had been cut down (by Lambert) and replaced. And the pleasant, rather than imposing, formal gardens that Badeslade shows had been laid out – a bowling green to the east, kitchen gardens defined by neat yew hedges, and gravel walks and lawns.

In the 1760s and 1770s this was all swept away when William Emes, a pupil of Capability Brown, landscaped the park and created an informal pleasure ground with woods and shrubberies enclosed by a ha-ha. Some of Emes' work survives – notably the little classical pavilion at the end of the long terrace – but most of the attractive five-acre gardens date mainly from the late nineteenth and early twentieth centuries.

Chirk's gardens date mainly from the late nineteenth and early twentieth centuries.

❖

'*I THINK THE CASTLE IS FITTED UP EXACTLY IN THAT STYLE OF ELEGANCE AND GRANDEUR, THAT BECOMES SO NOBLE A BUILDING, SO NOBLY SITUATED, & SHEWS GREAT TASTE.*'

John Henry Manners, *Journal of Three Years Travels* (1795)

❖

*Some of Emes's work is
still visible today — like
the classical pavilion at
the end of one terrace.*

WREST PARK
Bedfordshire

With Wrest, Earl de Grey was able to indulge his passion for French architecture: 'I had my French books always under my hand, [and] referred to them for authority whenever I could find anything to suit me.'

Kip's engraving of Wrest, which dates from circa 1702, shows the results of a radical remodelling carried out for the eleventh Earl of Kent in the late seventeenth century. From 1676 onwards the Earl began to transform the Tudor house that stood on the site, creating a rather grand rusticated entrance front to the north with a pedimented frontispiece and a cupola. (Large parts of the older building were retained, however; their chimneys and gables can be seen peeping over the dormers of the new façade.) The Earl also laid out the gardens in the 1680s and 1690s; Kip's view shows a central walk, aligned on the main axis of the north front and flanked by symmetrical parterres, leading through a grandiose pair of gates to a long, straight canal. A second canal ran off at forty-five degrees to the cross-axis of the formal garden and was balanced by a short avenue running north-east.

Although the eleventh Earl of Kent died in August 1702, the twelfth Earl continued his predecessor's improvements, bringing in Thomas Archer in 1709 to build the beautiful domed pavilion that now terminates the Long Water and

commissioning a series of designs from Giacomo Leoni in 1715 for a new house.

For some reason the designs were never executed. When Wrest was finally rebuilt between 1834 and 1839 on a site to the north of the original building, it was in a form far removed from Leoni's idiosyncratic brand of Palladianism. One could argue that for its time the style – a competent Louis XV – was a much more curious choice than anything Leoni might have produced. The man responsible for creating this château in the middle of the Bedfordshire countryside was its new owner, Thomas, Earl de Grey, an amateur architect who inherited the estate in 1833 and immediately began to indulge his passion for French architecture. 'I had my French books always under my hand', he wrote later, '[and] referred to them for authority whenever I could find anything to suit me.' That debt is acknowledged in the entrance hall, where the figure of Architecture holds books whose spines are inscribed with the names of Blondel, Mansart and Le Pautre.

Wrest Park c. 1702, drawn by Knyff and engraved by Kip shortly after being remodelled by the eleventh Earl of Kent.

'SOME ENCLOSED, WOODED GROUNDS BROUGHT ME TO THE HOUSE, WHERE, I SOUGHT, IN VAIN, FOR ADMISSION; AND AFTER A WAITING OF 20 MINUTES, (A SUFFICIENT TIME FOR A VIEW) WAS REFUSED BY THE SERVANTS... I DID, TO BE SURE, FEEL A LITTLE VEX'D — BUT WHAT CAN BE SEEN IN SUCH AN UGLY, MODERN HOUSE?'

John Byng, *A Tour in the Midlands* (1790)

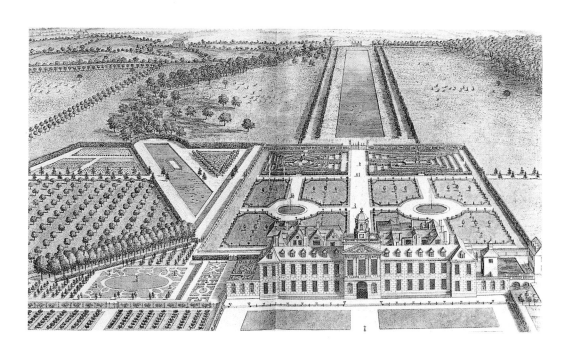

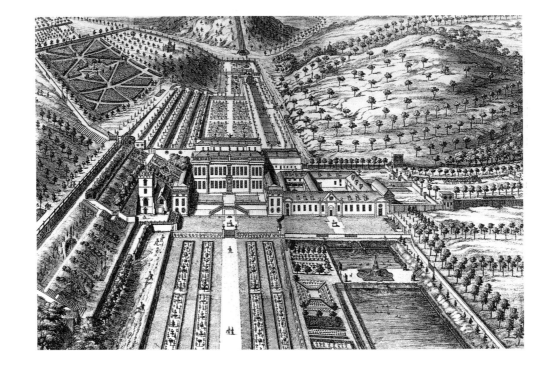

Kip's 1712 view of Dyrham, one of the finest Baroque gardens in England.

'ON YOUR
APPROACH TO THE
HOUSE FROM THE
HILLS, YOU ARE
AT ONCE
ENTERTAIN'D
WITH AN INFINITE
VARIETY OF
BEAUTIFUL
PROSPECTS.'
Stephen Switzer,
Icnographia Rustica

DYRHAM PARK
Avon

Like so many country houses, Dyrham Park owes its existence to a timely marriage. In September 1686 an ambitious government official named William Blathwayt was introduced to Mary Wynter, a thirty-six-year-old heiress whose father owned a tumbledown Tudor house in Gloucestershire. Although he initially showed little enthusiasm for the match (he was worried at the money he would have to lay out on new linen and plate), a visit to Dyrham – and a survey of the Wynter estates – convinced Blathwayt that Mary was the girl for him.

The investment in linen and plate paid off. By the end of 1691, Blathwayt's father-in-law, mother-in-law and wife had all died, leaving him with two sons and a daughter – as well as a 1700-acre country estate. He immediately set about turning the old house and its small garden into something more appropriate for a rising political star whose knowledge of Dutch, acquired during diplomatic service in The Hague as a young man, was making him one of William III's most trusted advisers.

The building was remodelled in two stages. Early in 1692 Samuel Hauderoy was commissioned to design a two-storey range to the west of the Tudor great hall. Six years later William Talman, one of the leading country house architects of the day, was brought in to build a second range to the east, containing state apartments with a single-storey orangery attached. A complex of stables and nurseries to the south, grouped around two courtyards, completed the house.

At the same time, Blathwayt's workmen were busy creating a spectacular formal setting for the new Dyrham. Natural springs in the park were diverted and dammed to provide water for fountains and a 224-step cascade, the noise of which, according to a contemporary, 'very near equals the Billows of a raging Sea'. There were avenues, canals and

parterres filled with orange trees, lemons and bays in tubs. Above a series of terraces to the north, a rectangular garden at the heart of a highly artificial 'Wilderness' held seats fitted with reading desks, causing one visitor to comment: 'I never in my whole Life did see so agreeable a Place for the sublimest Studies, as this is in the Summer.'

Blathwayt was to have more leisure to enjoy his new creation than he would have wished. With the death of

William III in 1702 he fell from favour at court. One by one his various posts were taken away until, angry and disillusioned, he retired to Dyrham, where he died in 1717.

His house has survived relatively unaltered, but the pleasure grounds had already fallen into neglect and decay by the 1770s. In 1791 they were described as 'now reconciled to modern Taste' — an inadequate euphemism to describe the destruction of one of the finest Baroque gardens in England.

Dyrham, 'now reconciled to modern Taste'.

*'A RURAL GARDEN...PERHAPS
EQUALLY BEAUTIFUL TO MOST WE
HAVE IN ENGLAND,
NOTWITHSTANDING THE HAPPY
POSSESSOR BEARS NO HIGHER
CHARACTER THAN THAT OF A
PRIVATE GENTLEMAN.'*

Stephen Switzer, *Icnographia Rustica* (1718)

*Samuel Hauderoy's west
front of 1692-4, with
William Talman's stable
block to the right.*

*Talman's east front and
single-storey orangery,
from a lithograph by
Hullmandel, c. 1835.*

HAMPTON COURT
Surrey

When Johannes Kip's engraving of Hampton Court was published at the end of the seventeenth century, the sprawling complex of Tudor buildings beside the Thames had just had a narrow escape. If Christopher Wren had had his way, the house in which Henry VIII had entertained each of his six wives, where Edward VI was born and Charles I held prisoner, would have been demolished. Within weeks of William and Mary's coronation in 1689, the couple decided to make Hampton Court a principal residence, and the Surveyor-General was drawing up plans for a magnificent palace to rival Versailles, an architectural statement that would declare the power and prestige of the new monarchs and confirm their right to govern.

In the event, a shortage of money and the death in 1694 of Queen Mary meant that Wren's scheme was never fully implemented, and the Tudor buildings grouped round the two courtyards closest to the river survived. But Wren did replace a third court, containing the old royal lodgings, with a set of state and private apartments. If his rather subdued Fountain Court is no match for the scale and grandeur of Versailles, it does at least draw strength from its dazzling setting – the Long Water and the three great lime avenues that radiate from the centre of Wren's garden front and that dominate Kip's view.

Inevitably, changes have been made to the grounds since William and Mary's time. The huge parterre containing fountains, statues and elaborately scrolled box hedges, which once filled the semicircle on the park front, has given way to lawns (reputedly at the command of Queen Anne, who disliked the smell of box). The intricate privy garden leading from Wren's east front down to the Thames has long since succumbed to later planting. But enough remains to ensure that Hampton Court is remembered, not as the Versailles that never was but as a rare and wonderful survival of the great age of Baroque design.

Hampton Court from the west.

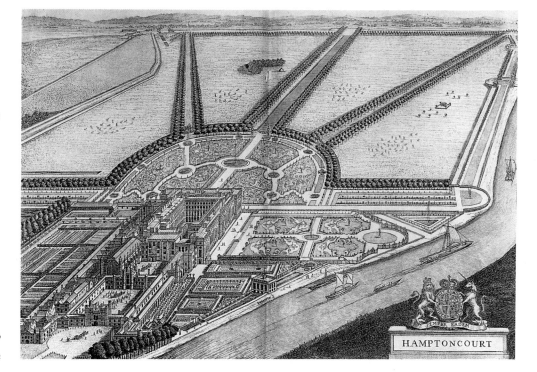

The box hedges which filled the semicircular parterre on the park front were replaced by lawn in the early eighteenth century, reputedly because Queen Anne disliked the smell of box. (Engraving by Kip, c. 1712)

❖

'THE GARDENS WERE DESIGNED TO BE VERY FINE, GREAT FOUNTAINES AND GRASS PLOTTS AND GRAVELL WALKES AND JUST AGAINST THE MIDDLE OF THE HOUSE WAS A VERY LARGE FOUNTAINE AND BEYOND IT A LARGE CANNAL GUARDED BY ROWS OF EVEN TREES THAT RUNN A GOOD WAY.'
Celia Fiennes, 'Hampton Court' (c. 1696)

❖

Thomas Robins's 1748
view of Benjamin Hyett's
six-acre Rococo gardens.

PAINSWICK HOUSE
Gloucestershire

For most of the eighteenth century the villa that Charles Hyett built for himself at Painswick between 1733 and 1738 was rather charmingly called Buenos Ayres – not because of any romantic attachment to South America but because the spot had a reputation for healthy air.

Hyett's house was interesting enough, but hardly an architectural masterpiece. It is to his son Benjamin, who succeeded him in 1738, that we owe the chief glory of Painswick House: its beautiful Rococo pleasure grounds. Laid out between 1738 and 1748, Benjamin's gardens occupied just six acres in the valley behind the house. Thomas Robins's painting, one of a set made the year they were finished, shows them in all their glorious detail. The landscape, strangely tilted so that it forms a backdrop to the house, contains a wealth of garden buildings, many in the delightful mid-eighteenth-century Gothick style whose disregard for medieval precedent is only

surpassed by its sheer joy. There is a spiky exedra at the end of the main axis, a rustic grotto, pavilions, pools and summer houses. A lead statue of Pan by Van Nost presided over the scene – a suitably impish deity for such a garden. His presence is apparently a memento of the decidedly Rococo idea that the name Painswick was actually a corruption of 'Pan's Wyck'.

Benjamin Hyett's garden survives. Unbelievably – and uniquely – it did not fall a victim to changing tastes. In spite of some modifications, its essential outlines still remained in the 1880s, but by the present century scrub and elder had hidden most of its features. In 1955 the estate passed to Lord Dickinson, a descendant of the Hyetts. Unaware that the garden still existed somewhere in the undergrowth, he filled the valley with a conifer plantation.

But research in the 1970s made the link between Robins's paintings and the various garden buildings half hidden in the woods. In 1984 Lord Dickinson made the difficult decision to

restore the eighteenth-century pleasure grounds to the state in which Robins had depicted them. Hedges and vistas have been replanted, using only species that would have been known to Benjamin Hyett in the 1740s. Buildings have

been rescued or reinstated using Robins's pictures. The painstaking reconstruction of the last surviving Rococo garden continues today under the aegis of a charitable trust set up in 1988.

The gardens today — a unique and delightful survival.

WILTON HOUSE
Wiltshire

Visitors have flocked to Wilton ever since the 1630s, when the fourth Earl of Pembroke commissioned the Frenchman Isaac de Caus to remodel the south front of his house – reputedly with help from Inigo Jones – and to create an elaborate formal garden, a thousand feet long and four hundred feet wide, beyond it.

A rather grandiose scheme for the house, which involved two state apartments and a vast, twenty-one bay façade, was probably intended to provide accommodation for Charles I, who was a frequent visitor to Wilton. When Pembroke sided with Parliament in the run-up to the Civil War, the King quite naturally ceased to call, and the plan was never fully implemented. A fire in the late 1640s led to John Webb being called in to redecorate the interiors from 1648 to 1650, again with the aid of Inigo Jones.

De Caus' grounds fared rather better. He was primarily a designer of gardens and waterworks and specialized in grottos – those at Jones's Banqueting House in Whitehall (1623-4), Woburn Abbey (1630) and Somerset House (1630-4) are a

The grounds have undergone a number of changes since the seventeenth century.

The south front, designed by Isaac de Caus in the 1630s and remodelled after a fire by John Webb between 1648 and 1650.

❖

'NO EXPENCE HAS BEEN SPARED, NO INGENUITY WANTING, TO RENDER IT THE MOST SUPERB EDIFICE IN ENGLAND.'

Dr E. D. Clarke, *A Tour Through the South of England* (1793)

❖

few documented examples, although only Woburn survives – and his gardens at Wilton were to become famous throughout the country.

Aubrey admired 'this magnificent garden and grotto', and 'that side of the house that fronts the garden, with two stately pavilions at each end, all al Italiano'. In 1654 John Evelyn noted that the gardens were 'esteem'd the noblest in England', and thirty years later Celia Fiennes described in minute detail the walks and statues. She was particularly enamoured of the grotto filled with sea-gods and water-tricks that faced the house: 'in one room [the water] makes the melody of Nightingerlls and all sorts of birds which engaged the curiosity of the Strangers to go in to see, but at the entrance off each room, is a line of pipes that appear not till by a sluce moved it washes the spectators.'

This interest continued into the eighteenth century. Mrs Lybbe Powys in 1776 observed, 'few persons pass by Wilton, as in the porter's lodge, where he desired us to set down our names and the number of our company, we saw by the book there had been to see it the last year 2324 persons'. Such was the demand for information about the house and its grounds that twenty-six editions of four different guidebooks were printed between 1751 and 1798 – one of which, *The Copious and Comprehensive Catalogue of the Curiosities of Wilton-House*, ran to a daunting 150 pages.

'To attempt a minute description would not only be absurd, but on my part impossible', wrote one tourist in 1791.

De Caus's famous gardens had gone by this time. They were landscaped by the ninth Earl of Pembroke between 1732 and 1738. The beautiful bridge, based on one of Palladio's drawings, was designed in 1737 by the Earl and his architect Roger Morris. To the west of the house, the loggia in the nineteenth-century Italian Garden incorporates fragments from the grotto admired so much by Celia Fiennes.

The grounds were landscaped and the Palladian Bridge built between 1732 and 1738 by the Earl of Pembroke and Roger Morris.

T E M P L E   N E W S A M
West Yorkshire

The first house at Temple Newsam was built in the early sixteenth century by Thomas, Lord Darcy, whose involvement with the Pilgrimage of Grace lost him his head in 1537. The estate, with its traditional diapered brick buildings on four sides of a courtyard, went to the Earl of Lennox and his wife, Margaret, niece of Henry VIII. Their son Lord Darnley, who was to marry Mary Queen of Scots, father James I and be murdered at Kirk o'Field – all before his twenty-first birthday – was born there in 1546.

In 1622 the Lennoxes sold Temple Newsam to a wealthy financier, Sir Arthur Ingram, and he is largely responsible for

In June 1699 the third Viscount Irwin paid Knyff £10 for 'taking the prospect of the Hall'.

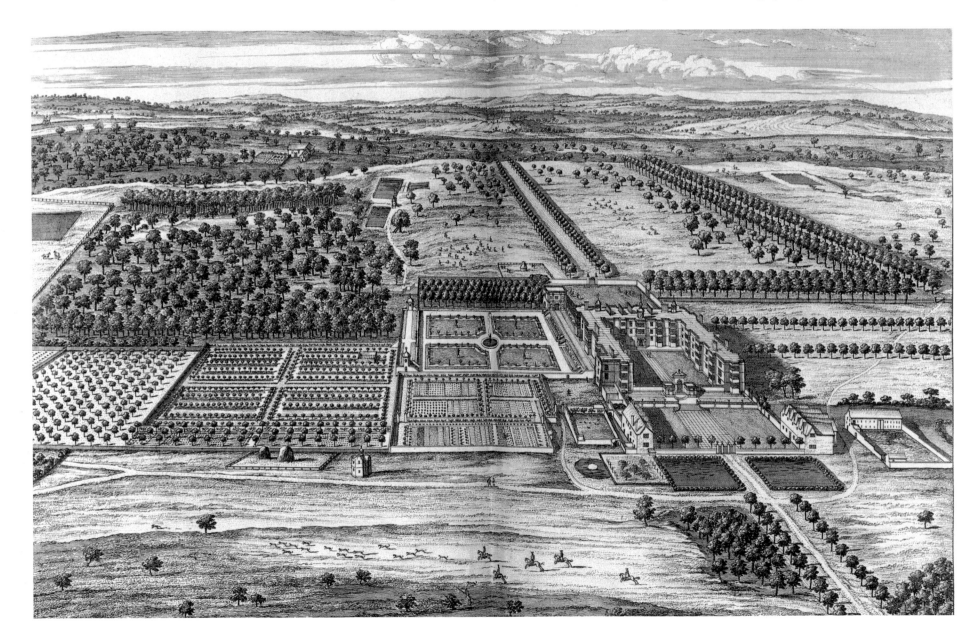

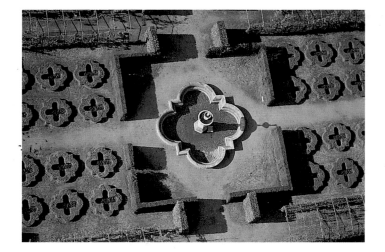

The present gardens are modern.

brought in William Etty of York to create a less rigid layout. In 1762 Capability Brown landscaped the park with serpentine walks, ha-has and picturesque eye-catchers, including a sham bridge and a rustic dairy. A Palladian stable court, probably designed by Lord Burlington's protégé Daniel Garrett, was put up to the north-east in 1740. In 1796 a Leeds architect named Thomas Johnson, whose father William had worked as agent and surveyor to the Irwins, totally rebuilt the south wing of the house, changing its three storeys to two but otherwise staying remarkably faithful to Arthur Ingram's original Caroline conception. The present 'Victorian' and 'Elizabethan' gardens are modern.

Although Thomas Johnson rebuilt the south wing (to the left in the picture) in 1796, he remained remarkably faithful to the original seventeenth-century conception.

its appearance today. Shortly after buying the house he razed the east wing and rebuilt the north and south ranges to form the present U-shaped plan. He also added the grand entrance porch and Temple Newsam's most famous feature — the balustrade of open lettering which runs around the roof: ALL GLORY AND PRAISE BE GIVEN TO GOD THE FATHER THE SON AND HOLY GHOST ON HIGH PEACE ON EARTH GOOD WILL TOWARDS MEN HONOUR AND TRUE ALLEGIANCE TO OUR GRACIOUS KING LOVING AFFECTION AMONGST HIS SUBJECTS HEALTH AND PLENTY BE WITHIN THIS HOUSE.

Knyff's view of Temple Newsam can be dated quite precisely; in June 1699 the third Viscount Irwin, a descendant of Ingram, paid him £10 for 'taking the prospect of the Hall'. (He clearly approved the artist's work, commissioning his own portrait from him the following year.) The formal gardens, laid out for Sir Arthur Ingram by Peter Monjoye, included a large parterre to the south of the house with beds, gravel walks and topiary; a raised walk culminating in an appealing banqueting house; a corresponding raised terrace on the south side of the parterre, with little octagonal pavilions at either end; and a bowling green to the west, behind the Tudor range. An architectural screen linked the two wings and gave onto an outer court flanked by two service blocks.

Sadly, this has all disappeared. In 1710 the third Viscount

The park, landscaped by Capability Brown in 1762. Leeds looms in the background.

CHAPTER THREE

Who was responsible for designing a country house?

The obvious answer, of course, is 'the architect'. His name (and in the context of the English country house, it was almost certain to be a 'he') may have long been forgotten. We simply don't know, for example, who was responsible for Groombridge or Broome Park or Penshurst or Athelhampton, but even when we don't know his identity, surely we can be certain that someone, somewhere, sat down with a piece of paper and produced a detailed design that was implemented by a team of masons and joiners and labourers. Otherwise, how would the thing come to be built at all?

But the issue isn't that straightforward. Most of the country houses in this book didn't have an architect in the way that we understand the word today, for the simple reason that well into the eighteenth century, the idea of the professional architect didn't exist. A Greek-Latin-French-English dictionary published in 1580 could find no real English equivalents for 'architectus' or 'architector', coming up instead with 'the maister mason, the maister carpenter, or the principall overseer and contriver of any work'. As late as 1708 William Talman, whom we would certainly describe as the architect of the south and east fronts of Chatsworth – and who was eager to confirm his status at every possible opportunity – described himself not as architect but as 'chief overseer and surveyor' to the Duke of Devonshire.

The fact was that there was no professional training in architecture until the later eighteenth century,

PERSONAL STATEMENTS

✤

OWNERS,
ARCHITECTS AND OTHER
ECCENTRICS

Jan Siberechts's spectacular painting of Wollaton Hall, dated 1697, captures the house and its grounds in its magnificence.

when successful architects like Sir Robert Taylor and James Paine pioneered the practice of taking on pupils who served a five- or six-year apprenticeship while perhaps attending lectures at the Royal Academy. Previous to this even the King's Works, the country's leading building office and probably the most important national focus for the advancement of architectural design, was sometimes headed by men with no experience in architecture at all. The post of Surveyor-General of the Works, which was held by Inigo Jones and Sir Christopher Wren, was also occupied for nine years (from 1660 to 1669) by the cavalier-poet Sir John Denham, who didn't design a single building. Though he may 'have some knowledge of the theory of architecture', wrote John Webb, 'he can have none of the practice, but must employ another'. Sir Thomas Hewitt, who held the post from 1719 to 1726, was responsible on-

ly for a temple in his own gardens and a stable-block in Nottinghamshire, characterized by Hawksmoor as 'the only piece of Building that Sr Tho Hewett was Guilty of, during his being Architect Royall . . . [and] the most infamous that ever was made'.

During the sixteenth and seventeenth centuries, the designs for country houses were produced by craftsmen in the building trades (as they had been throughout the Middle Ages), by gentlemen-amateurs, or by the clients themselves. Those clients discussed the projects with their peers, examined each other's drawings and plans, packed off their masons and surveyors to study each other's houses and offered and received advice and criticism. When Hardwick Hall was being built, for example, Bess of Hardwick visited Wollaton and Holdenby in 1592, presumably on the lookout for ideas. Holdenby's owner, Sir Christopher Hatton, invited

> *PLANS AND ELEVATIONS WERE REGULARLY MODIFIED IN EXECUTION, SOMETIMES AT THE BEHEST OF THE CLIENT, BUT MORE OFTEN AS A RESULT OF THE IDEAS AND EXPERIENCE OF THE MASONS AND CARPENTERS WHO WORKED ON THEM.*

William Cecil's criticisms of his new house, since 'as the same is done hitherto in direct observation of your house and plots of Theobalds, so I earnestly pray your Lordship that by your good corrections at this time, it may appear as like to the same as it hath ever been meant to be'. And the first Duke of Devonshire's constant in-terference in the design of Chatsworth in the 1680s and 1690s culmi-nated in labour disputes and a number of law suits with his builders.

Mention of the Duke of Devonshire's all-too-direct involvement in the building work at Chatsworth brings up another com-plicating factor in assigning personal responsibility for a creation as complex as a country house. Plans and elevations were regularly modified in execution, sometimes at the behest of the client, but more often as a result of the ideas and experience of the masons and carpenters who worked on them, while decora-tive schemes were produced by the plasterworkers and carvers rather than by the 'architect'.

Longleat, for example, was very much a collabora-tive effort. It underwent a series of dramatic transfor-mations between 1547, when Sir John Thynne began to convert the monastery buildings on the site in-to a home for himself, and his death in 1580. Thynne was actively in-volved in at least part of the design. A contract of 1559 specifies that some new work was to be put up 'according to a platt thereof made and signed by the said Sir John Thynne and William Spicer'. (Spicer was one of the masons involved in the building.) After a fire in 1567, a French joiner named Adrian Gaunt was paid for 'making ye modell for ye house of Longleate', and be-tween 1572 and 1580 two master masons, Alan Maynard and Robert Smythson, were working on the final designs, with constant advice from Thynne him-

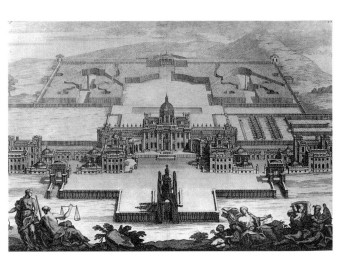

Castle Howard was John Vanbrugh's first commis-sion. Swift remarked, 'Van's genius, without thought or lecture / Is hugely turn'ed to architecture'.

self. In all this work the craftsmen – masons, joiners and carvers – worked in virtually independent gangs, using drawings as the basis for their creations but not hesitating to alter them in greater or lesser detail as they saw fit.

A hundred years later the situation was much the same. Sir John Brown-low, the owner of Belton House (1685-8), almost certainly commissioned drawings from Captain William Winde, a pro-fessional soldier who had fought against Mon-mouth's rebels at Sedge-moor in 1685 and whose interest in military engineering led him to supple-ment his income by dabbling in country-house ar-chitecture. Winde would simply have provided Brownlow with a roughly drawn outline design. The work of implementing the design was left to a mason-contractor named William Stanton who, like Winde, had other strings to his bow: he was primarily a mon-

A COUNTRY HOUSE — ANY WORK OF ARCHITECTURE, IN FACT — IS THE PRODUCT OF A WHOLE NETWORK OF PERSONAL, SOCIAL AND CULTURAL FORCES THAT COME TOGETHER ONLY ONCE TO CREATE SOMETHING UNIQUE.

umental sculptor, who had come to the family's notice in 1681 when he set up a funerary monument to Brownlow's great-uncle in Belton church. Here again the various craftsmen – plasterworker Edward Goudge, decorative carver Edmund Carpenter, joiner Edward Willcox – would have designed the details.

❖ ❖ ❖

So to what extent can we really say that any of the country houses in this chapter – or, indeed, any country house built before the architectural profession was estab-lished in the mid-eigh-teenth century – was really a personal statement, a reflection of one indi-vidual mind?

With hindsight, it is easy to find reasons for the choice of a style, the treatment of a single element. Looking back at James Wyatt's Belvoir Castle (1800-25), for example, social and architectural historians can nod knowingly and talk about the

French Revolution and the fears that it produced in the English landed classes, about how the spate of castle building that took place in this period was an expression of those fears. No doubt they are right. But it is hard to imagine the young Duke of Rutland sitting down with Wyatt and saying, 'It could happen here, y'know. I need to show the hoi polloi who's boss. Build me a castle.' A country house — any work of architecture, in fact — is more multifaceted than that; it is the product of a whole network of personal, social and cultural forces that come together once to create something unique.

Yet country houses are about people. The application of stylistic labels and the discussion of cultural trends can help us to understand the buildings, but if we ignore the contribution of individuals — each of which is as unique as the architecture itself — we miss the point. It is impossible to look at Wollaton Hall in

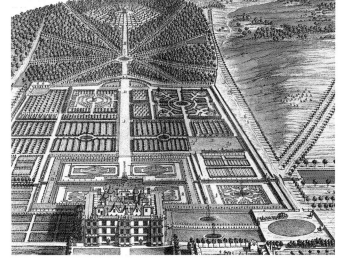

all its flamboyant eccentricity without speculating about its equally eccentric owner. We can't admire Chatsworth without calling to mind the authoritarian first Duke of Devonshire spending his workmen's wages on the horses, or Ashdown without thinking of the Earl of Craven in mourning for the Winter Queen. Such people gave life to the country houses in this chapter and are the thread that links them together.

We should bear in mind that there were other players in the cast beyond the owners, beyond even the craftsmen and designers. The building of a country house has always been a collective project, and while we remember Maynard and Smythson and Gaunt at Longleat, or Stanton and Winde at Belton, or Wyatt at Belvoir, let us not forget the men and women who cleared the site and carted the stone and gathered the fuel for the brick kilns. These houses are their creation, too.

Much of Longleat's grounds are now a safari park.

L O N G L E A T
Wiltshire

The first of the great Elizabethan prodigy houses, Longleat remains the most imposing – a supreme expression of the energy and confidence with which so many Tudor courtiers grasped everything within reach, convinced of their ability to turn it to gold.

The man behind the creation of Longleat was Sir John Thynne, who paid £53 for the medieval priory that stood on the site in 1540. Thynne belonged to a powerful group of cultured Protestant politicians, merchants and bankers who gathered around Lord Protector Somerset and who managed by one means or another to hang on to their heads and their

Longleat and its grounds c. 1700, drawn by Knyff and engraved by Kip. The gardens were laid out by London and Wise at the end of the seventeenth century.

estates during Mary's Counter-Reformation before rising again during the reign of Elizabeth. His friends included William Cecil and Thomas Smith, both Secretaries of State; his wife was sister to Sir Thomas Gresham, the financier who founded the Royal Exchange.

But Thynne was neither a politician nor a financier. In spite of his influential connections, he preferred to devote his life to building. From the mid-1540s, when he began to convert the monastic complex into lodgings for his family and household, until his death in 1580, by which time he had created four different Longleats, each one grander than the

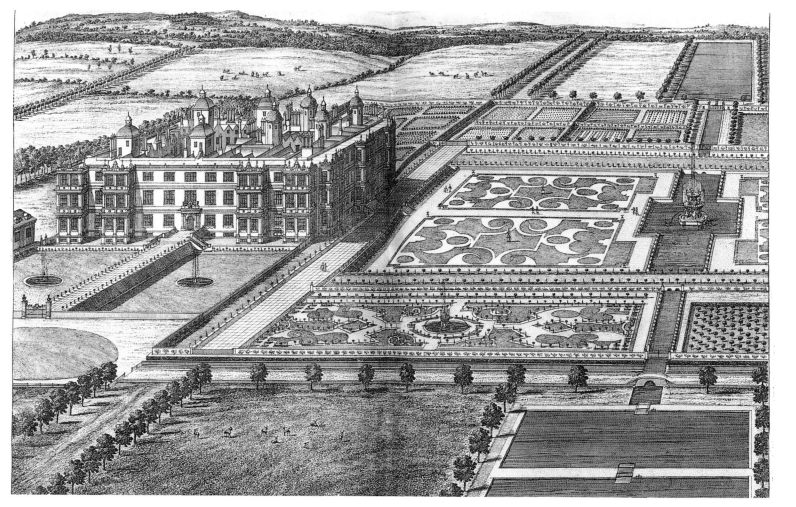

'IN PASSING THROUGH THE GROUNDS OF LORD WEYMOUTH, ONE IS FURTHER SURPRIZED AT THE VAST CAPABILITIES WHICH THEY POSSESS... TREES INDEED IN CLUMPS ARE ALREADY PLANTING, AND IN TIME IT IS PROBABLE THE OLD CANALS, THE MOST GLARING VESTIGES OF EXPLODED TASTE, WILL BE EITHER TURNED INTO MORE NATURAL FORMS OR BE ENTIRELY FILLED UP.'

Richard Sulivan, *Observations on England, Scotland and Wales* (1780)

last, his aspirations grew, and his reach gradually extended to gather in the most talented masons and carpenters of his day.

The result was – is – breathtaking. With its symmetrical façades, expanses of glass and use of classical detail, Longleat is a world away from traditional early-Tudor houses, their lodgings and domestic offices huddled defensively round a central courtyard. Unlike those houses, it looks out confidently on the world, proclaiming its owner's status and wealth, daring anyone to disagree.

Little is known about the gardens with which Sir John Thynne chose to surround his new house, although his close involvement in every phase of the building process suggests that they too bore the stamp of his personality. The grounds shown in Kip's engraving were largely laid out by the royal gardeners London and Wise at the end of the seventeenth century. Their parterres and formal canals were swept away by Capability Brown and Humphry Repton, who were responsible for the landscape that is there today.

At Longleat Sir John Thynne brought together many of the most talented craftsmen of his day.

A supreme expression of the energy and confidence with which Tudor courtiers grasped everything within reach, convinced of their ability to turn it into gold.

Brown and Repton swept away the formal gardens. The canals were turned into a meandering river.

Longleat c. 1700, by Jan Siberechts.

BELTON HOUSE
Lincolnshire

When Sir John Brownlow entertained William III at Belton in 1695 and the King 'made merry and drank freely . . . [so] that when he came to Lincoln he could eat nothing but a mess of milk', it must have seemed to onlookers that nothing could go wrong for the young country squire. Money, political influence, good luck – Brownlow had it all.

In 1676, only sixteen years old, he had married his cousin Alice, uniting two branches of the family and thereby ensuring that his childless great-uncle would settle his huge fortune on the young man. The great-uncle died three years later, and Sir John inherited estates in Lincolnshire, £20,000 in ready money and an annual income of around £9,000. By the early 1680s he and Alice had launched themselves into London society, spending £5,000 on a town house in Southampton Square, one of the most fashionable addresses in the capital. Inevitably, he decided to rebuild the family's country house at Belton, just outside Grantham.

Begun in 1684, the design for Belton was almost certainly provided by the gifted gentleman-architect William Winde, though in line with normal Caroline building practice, the execution was entrusted to a mason-contractor, William Stanton.

But another figure hovers over Belton. Winde's design was heavily influenced by the great palace that his contemporary Roger Pratt created for the Earl of Clarendon in Piccadilly between 1664 and 1667. Much of its success derives from the same elegant combination of elements that Winde and Brownlow must have seen at Clarendon House before it was demolished in 1683. Like Clarendon, Belton is a two-storey block with a central pediment between projecting wings; like Clarendon, it has a hipped roof with broad eaves, dormer windows with alternating triangular and segmental pediments; and like Clarendon, its roof is surmounted by a balustraded platform crowned with a cupola. Pratt's mansion was to be the model for many gentry houses during the later seventeenth century, but nowhere was it so successfully recreated as at Belton.

Sir John Brownlow moved into his new home in 1688 and continued his successful career as a wealthy landed gentleman. He became MP for Grantham. He was High Sheriff of Lincolnshire. And, in spite of the hangover, King William was so pleased with his visit that he summoned Brownlow to London to thank him personally. Everything seemed set for the next step – elevation to the peerage.

Brownlow never took that step. In 1697 a contemporary recorded that 'Sir John Brownlow member of Parliament for Grantham . . . last week shot himself at Mr Freake's [his uncle's house] in Dorsetshire, but the reason not known.'

An eighteenth-century bird's-eye of Belton by Thomas Smith.

A hangover from the past – William III got so drunk at Belton that the next day he could eat nothing but 'a mess of milk'.

'AND THEN, HOW THE GROUND-SURFACE IS
GEMMED WITH EVERYTHING WHICH MAY RIVET
THE ATTENTION, AND DELIGHT THE
IMAGINATION — FOR HERE YOU SHALL FANCY
THE FAIRIES TO RESORT BY MOONLIGHT; NOW
SKIMMING OVER THE PELLUCID FOUNTAIN IN
THE CENTRE, NOW REVELLING UPON THE
ADJACENT LAWN, AND NOW REPOSING WITHIN
THE RESPLENDENT CACTUS, PROTECTED BY ITS
CURTAINS OF SCARLET VELVET, AND ITS
FRINGES OF DEEP VIRGIN GOLD.'

Rev. T. F. Dibdin, *A Bibliographical, Antiquarian and
Picturesque Tour* (1838)

*Heavily influenced by
Roger Pratt's Clarendon
House, Piccadilly, Belton
is perhaps the finest
country house of its type
to survive today.*

*Wealth, power and luck
– Sir John Brownlow, the
builder of Belton, had it
all. But only nine years
after his new house was
completed, Brownlow shot
himself.*

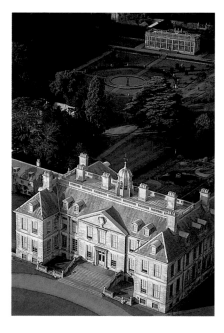

WOLLATON HALL
Nottinghamshire

The history of the English country house is liberally sprinkled with eccentrics. Francis Willoughby, the builder of Wollaton Hall, is one of the most colourful.

A wealthy landowner, Willoughby responded enthusiastically to the entrepreneurial spirit of the age, mining coal on a huge scale and investing in ironworks, shipping and glass. He was well read, cultured and a devout if strange Protestant who wrote sermons for his own chaplain to preach to him. In his library was a Life of St Thomas Becket in which every reference to the Pope has been carefully deleted. He was also deeply suspicious of both friends and family; his first wife left him after ten years of marriage, tired of his paranoid persecution. However, that paranoia seems to have had some roots in reality where his second wife was concerned: she was described by a contemporary as a 'whore . . . [who] stripped him both of goods and lands and left him nothing but what hangs upon his back'.

In 1580 Robert Smythson, who worked at Wardour Castle in Wiltshire for Willoughby's brother-in-law Matthew Arundell, was employed to build a new house at Wollaton, a house that was to be no less picturesque than its owner. Drawing for the plan and much of the ornament on European pattern books, including Sebastiano Serlio's *L'Architettura* and works by Vredeman de Vries and Jacques Androuet du Cerceau, Smythson tempered the ensemble with a dash of English Gothic so strong that Wollaton from afar resembles nothing so much as a fairy-tale castle, with corner towers and a great keep rising above high curtain walls. But the walls are made of glass. The towers are capped not with crenellations and embrasures but with strapwork cresting, obelisks and clusters of chimneys. And the 'keep' is in fact a massive central hall lit by a clerestory and topped by a tourelled prospect room with magnificent views over the surrounding countryside – a belvedere rather than a watchtower, a lantern sending out its beams of stately and curious workmanship across the county.

The tourelled prospect room: a lantern sending out its beams of stately and curious workmanship across the county.

From a distance, Wollaton seems like a fairy-tale castle, with corner towers and a great keep rising high above curtain walls.

Knyff's early eighteenth-century view of Wollaton.

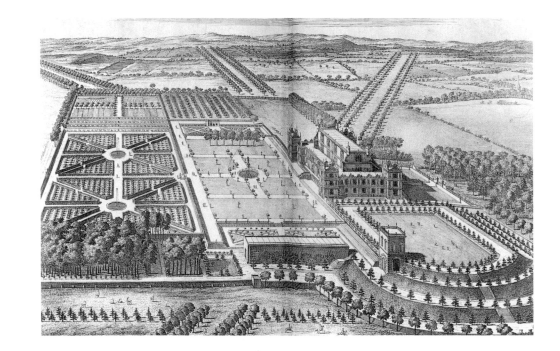

'*FROM NOTTINGHAM, A LITTLE MILE
WEST ON THE ROAD TO DERBY, WE SAW
WOOLLATON HALL, THE NOBLEST
ANTIENT-BUILT PALACE IN THIS
COUNTY...THE HOUSE, THE GARDENS,
THE GREAT HALL, THE MONUMENTS OF
THE FAMILY IN THE CHURCH OF
WOOLLATON, AND THE PEDIGREE OF
THAT NOBLE FAMILY, ARE WELL WORTH
A STRANGER'S VIEW.*'

Daniel Defoe, *A Tour Through England and Wales* (1726)

*A house no less
picturesque than
its owner.*

*Perched high on a hill,
Wollaton still dominates
the Nottingham
landscape.*

ASHDOWN HOUSE
Oxfordshire

The first Earl of Craven, builder of Ashdown House, first met Elizabeth of Bohemia in the late 1620s. The Winter Queen – so-called because her husband reigned as King of Bohemia for only one year before losing his throne – was living in exile in The Hague. Craven was a professional soldier serving under Prince Maurice of Orange. The meeting was to change his life.

From that point on, the Earl devoted himself to the Winter Queen's cause. When her husband's death in 1632 left her with few friends and little money, he became her champion, fighting for her, pleading her cause around Europe and doing everything he could to help her regain her property and fortune. It was Craven who raised £30,000 to fund a campaign led by her son, Prince Rupert, to recover his father's lands in Bohemia; Craven who provided her with money to fend off her creditors during the 1650s, when his own estates had been sequestrated by Parliament; Craven who brought her to England after the Restoration, placing his London house at her disposal.

So it is scarcely surprising that legend should link Ashdown with the Winter Queen. Craven is said to have intended the house as a refuge for Elizabeth from the plague that was sweeping London in the winter of 1661-2, but she died before he could complete it. Heartbroken, the Earl then consecrated the new house to her memory, remaining a bachelor until his own death thirty-five years later.

The date is right, but the motive is less romantic. Despite Craven's devotion to Elizabeth, Ashdown was designed not as a shrine to a queen but simply as a hunting lodge and country retreat. Standing at the junction of four rides through a wooded and impaled deer park, the house served as a sort of grandstand. From its upper storeys and balustraded roof spectators could watch the chase, and the Earl could stay here while hunting or when his main residence at nearby Hampstead Marshall was being

As if some giant hand has plucked a town house out of Amsterdam or The Hague and placed it in the English countryside.

given its annual spring cleaning.

If Ashdown's legends are open to question, its surreal beauty is not. Probably designed by William Winde (Craven's godson and another professional soldier who had served in the Netherlands), the building's compact square plan, tall proportions and steeply pitched roof punctuated by dormer windows and capped with a cupola combine to suggest that some giant hand has plucked a town house out of Amsterdam or The Hague and carefully placed it in the English countryside. The effect, only slightly diminished by the loss of the deer park, is startling even today; Ashdown remains a shrine – not to the Winter Queen but to one of the most exciting and attractive periods in the history of English architecture.

Ashdown in the early eighteenth century, a country retreat at the junction of four rides (Knyff and Kip, c. 1707).

An early-Victorian view
of Belvoir Castle by
Joseph Rhodes.

BELVOIR CASTLE
Leicestershire

The fifth Duke of Rutland was only twenty-two years old when in 1800 he and his young wife, Elizabeth, decided to modernize Belvoir Castle. It was long overdue: in June 1789 John Byng noted bitterly that 'every thing is in neglect, and Ruin, and in such a state it has long been . . . at present there is not an habitable Room, or a Bed fit to sleep in'.

Rutland's choice of architect was James Wyatt, Surveyor-General of the Office of Works. Wyatt was a talented designer in any style you cared to name, but his prolific output – more than two hundred projects in forty years – was equalled only by his irresponsibility. 'What putrid inn, what stinking tavern or pox-ridden brothel hides your hoary and gluttonous limbs?' demanded William Beckford, infuriated by

Wyatt's absence from Fonthill Abbey. Constantly pursued by, or in hiding from, irate clients, he was so rarely at his post as Surveyor-General that his cleaning woman ran a girls' school in his Whitehall office.

Despite that, the building works went smoothly for more than a decade. Wyatt produced one of his most spectacular essays in castellated Gothic, a style that gained a new significance during the early nineteenth century as an authoritarian gesture of defiance towards revolution across the Channel and agitation at home. His cheerful mixture of Norman and Gothic may not have been scholarly (Pugin was later to describe him as a 'monster of architectural depravity' for his equally cheerful approach to cathedral restoration), but his aim was visual impact rather than scholarship. Whatever else may be said about Belvoir, its towers and

turrets and battlements certainly have visual impact.

Wyatt has to share the credit for Belvoir, however. In 1813, before he could fall out with the Duke and just as various government agencies were closing in on him for his mismanagement of the Office of Works, he was killed in a timely carriage accident. Work continued on the house until October 1816, when a fire destroyed the northern half of the building and the Duke's chaplain, Sir John Thoroton, stepped in to design replacements. The projecting entrance to the north-west in his; so too is the tall principal tower and most of the rest of the north-west and north-east ranges, which are filled with borrowings from Lincoln Cathedral.

Whatever else one thinks of Belvoir, its towers and turrets and battlements certainly have visual impact.

There has been a castle at Belvoir since shortly after the Norman Conquest.

Badeslade's 1731 view shows the seventeenth-century Belvoir, with the site of the original Norman keep to the right.

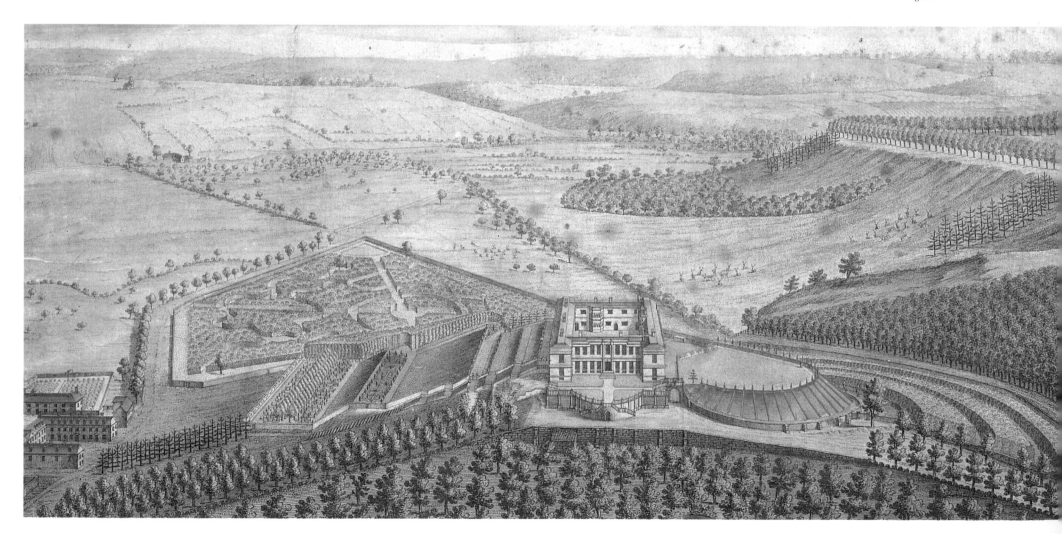

Although James Wyatt —
who with Sir John
Thoroton was responsible
for Belvoir as it stands
today — was a notoriously
difficult architect to work
with, his flair for
exploiting the picturesque
potential of a site was
unrivalled.

'AND NOW, THE NEARER YOU
APPROACH, THE MORE ELEVATED AND
IMPOSING THE CASTLE STANDS;
THROWING ITS TURRETS, AND
PINNACLES, AND BATTLEMENTS, HIGH
INTO AIR, OVER WHICH THE CLOUDS
WERE FLOATING IN FLEECY MAJESTY,
CASTING THEIR BROAD AND BROWN
SHADOWS BELOW.'

Rev. T. F. Dibdin, *A Bibliographical, Antiquarian and
Picturesque Tour* (1838)

One of Wyatt's most
spectacular essays in
castellated Gothic.

CHATSWORTH
Derbyshire

William Talman's south front, 1687-96: with its block-like elevation and long balustraded roofline, Talman's design marked a radical departure in English country house architecture.

When William Cavendish, fourth Earl of Devonshire, inherited Chatsworth in 1684, the house was substantially the same one that his great-great-grandmother, Bess of Hardwick, had put up more than a century earlier. It was clearly old-fashioned and inconvenient, but the Earl soon had more important things on his mind. Implacably opposed to absolutism and Catholicism, James II's accession in 1685 brought him into conflict with the Crown, and matters came to a head the following year,

when he manhandled one of James's courtiers at Whitehall. He was fined £40,000, and to avoid paying he retreated to his Derbyshire estate, where he continued to oppose the King, receiving a dukedom from William of Orange for his services during the Glorious Revolution.

It was during this enforced exile that Cavendish decided to remodel Chatsworth. William Talman and his master mason Benjamin Jackson were brought in to create a new south façade. Talman also remodelled the east front, though less successfully. In midsummer 1696, however, the relationship between the two men ended abruptly with Talman's dismissal. It is ironic that the champion of liberty and opponent of autocracy was himself supremely arrogant and autocratic in his personal dealings. He constantly changed his mind about the alterations; even after they were built, he expected his workmen to respond to his whims unquestioningly. By 1699 Jackson and his men had also downed their tools, exasperated that the Duke was slow to pay them while gambling thousands of pounds on the horses. His response was in character: he sacked them too.

It was at this point that Knyff was summoned to Chatsworth to draw Cavendish's new house, and his view shows what a curious mixture it must have been. In the midst of George London's formal gardens, the Elizabethan range and its two towers are clearly visible next to Talman's sophisticated south front.

The remains of Bess of Hardwick's house – the west and north façades – were replaced over the next eight years as the Duke pressed on with his improvements. He died in 1707, leaving the second Duke to settle the various lawsuits that the dismissed craftsmen had lodged. Large parts of London's formal gardens fell victim to Capability Brown in the eighteenth century, and in the nineteenth, the sixth Duke added the north wing, while his friend and head gardener Joseph Paxton laid out the grounds that are there today.

The Baroque west front, with the north wing added by the sixth Duke of Devonshire in the nineteenth century to the right, and stables (by James Paine, 1758-63) beyond.

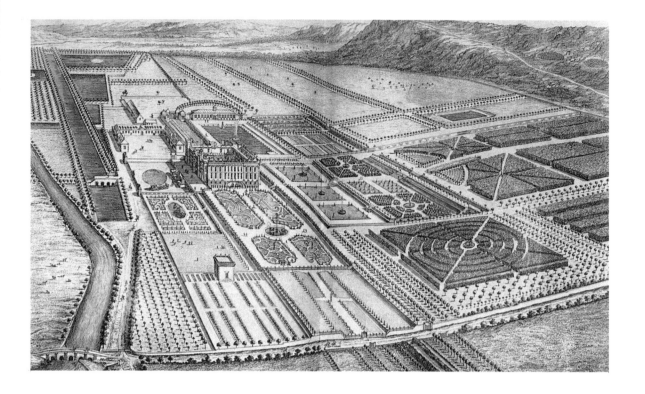

Knyff's view was taken
c. 1700, when
Chatsworth was still half
Elizabethan and half
Baroque.

❖

'THERE IS A LARGE PARKE AND SEVERALL FINE
GARDENS ONE WITHOUT ANOTHER WITH
GRAVELL WALKES AND SQUAIRS OF GRASS
WITH STONE STATUES IN THEM AND IN THE
MIDDLE OF EACH GARDEN IS A LARGE
FOUNTAINE FULL OF IMAGES SEA GODS AND
DOLPHINS AND SEA HORSES WHICH ARE FULL
OF PIPLES WHICH SPOUT OUT WATER IN THE
BASON AND SPOUTS ALL ABOUT THE GARDENS.'
Celia Fiennes, *My Northern Journey* (1697)

❖

George London's formal
gardens were swept away
by Capability Brown in
the eighteenth century.
Parts of the present
gardens were laid out by
Joseph Paxton in the
nineteenth.

CHAPTER FOUR

VISIONS OF ENGLAND

❖

*IMAGES OF
COUNTRY LIFE, IMAGES
OF THE PAST*

'Man is in love, and loves what vanishes,/What more is there to say?' In these two lines William Butler Yeats sums up the country house's most compelling appeal in the late twentieth century: it is an icon, a symbol of a world we have lost. Explore the galleries and halls of Penshurst or Ightham Mote, investigate the quiet charm of Groombridge Place or Athelhampton, and the aesthetic experience takes second place to the associations (either real or imagined – it makes little difference) that the buildings have with the past.

This wasn't always the case. Although in Tudor and Stuart times a few individuals had valued old buildings because they were old (Francis Bacon's declaration that 'it is a reverend thing to see an ancient castle or building not in decay' is a case in point), most people – insofar as they thought critically about country houses at all – were much more excited by modern architecture. In the 1580s Sir Francis Willoughby didn't think twice before abandoning his ancestral home at Wollaton in favour of a brand new house on a different site. A little more than a century later William Blathwayt had no qualms about demolishing most of the Elizabethan manor that stood at Dyrham, replacing it with a more up-to-date and convenient building. And the praise of contemporaries was likewise reserved for the latest thing. To the traveller in the reign of William and Mary or Queen Anne, the medieval Haddon Hall might be dismissed as merely 'a good old house . . . but nothing very curious as the mode now is'. Chatsworth, on the other hand, or Badminton or Castle Howard or any of the other great

Westwood Park, Hereford and Worcester. A hunting lodge built for Sir John Pakington at the end of the sixteenth century. It survives almost unchanged since Knyff's view was taken.

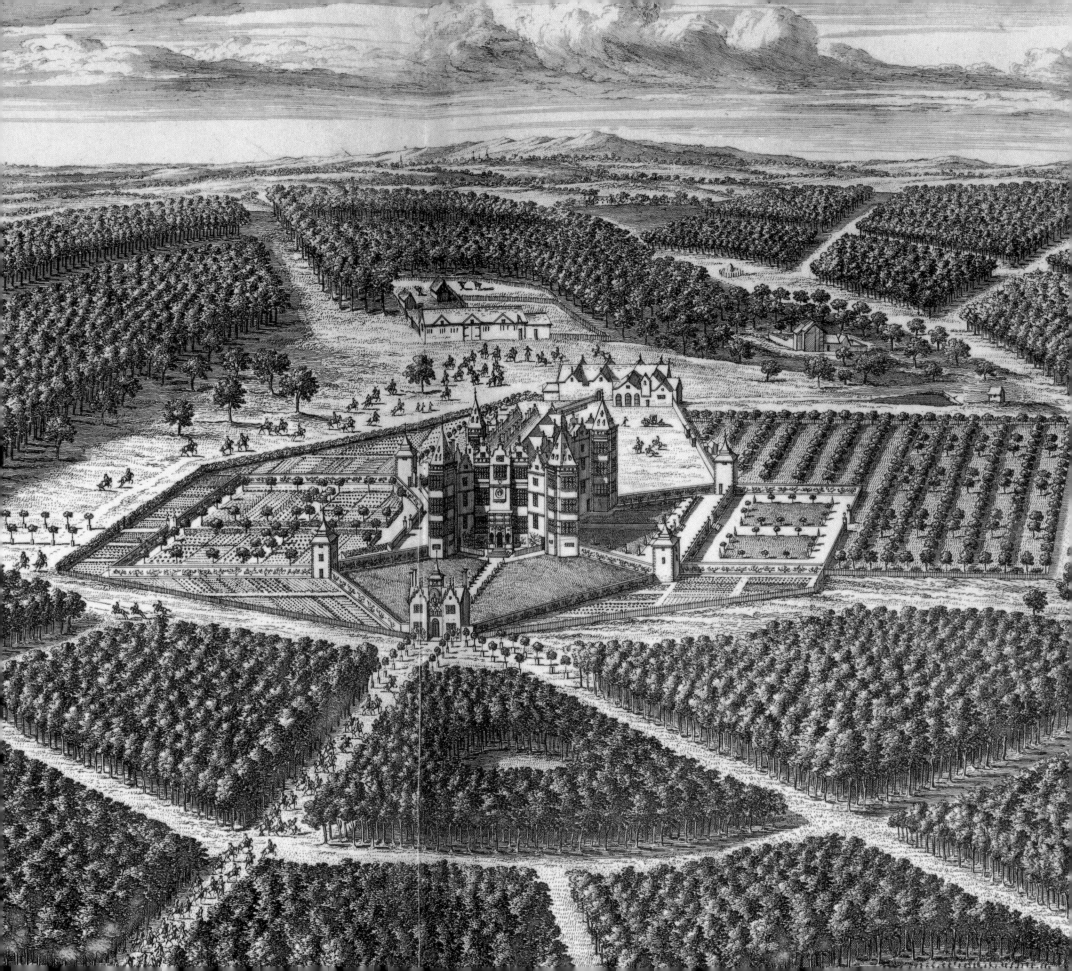

Baroque power houses, was exciting, stimulating and, above all, new.

There was always a certain nostalgia for the manners of the past, however. It was inextricably bound up with a mistrust of the present, and that nostalgia was easily transferred to the ancient buildings that seemed to form a bulwark against the tide of progress. Ben Jonson's poem 'To Penshurst' (1616) is perhaps the most famous early example of the way in which fashionably 'modern' mansions were compared unfavourably with older houses – 'their lords have built, but thy lord dwells' – but the literature of the seventeenth century is peppered with others, from Herrick and Marvell to Thomas Shadwell, who in his 1681 play *The Lancashire Witches* has Sir Edward Hartfort declare, ''Twas never good days but when great tables were kept in large halls, the buttery-hatch always open; black jacks, and a good smell of meat and March beer; with dogs' turds and marrow bones as ornaments in the hall . . . I hate to see Italian fine buildings with no meat or drink in 'em.'

The Gothick Revival of the eighteenth century offered an alternative to the 'Italian fine buildings' so contemptuously dismissed by Shadwell. From Sanderson Miller, Henry Keene and Horace Walpole, polite society learned that the buildings of the past – our native past rather than classical Rome or Renaissance Italy – could provide an inspiration for new architecture. Hand in hand with the Gothick of Strawberry Hill went an interest in the architecture of the Middle Ages: 'I never enter a noble old hall,' wrote an anonymous traveller in 1789, 'without seeing in my imagination the Baron feasting merrily with his Knights . . . When I proceed, and see the walls of the gallery adorned with the court of Harry, Elizabeth, or James, I am overwhelmed by my feelings.'

THE NAPOLEONIC WARS, AS WELL, LED TO A CURTAILMENT OF THE GRAND TOUR OF EUROPE AND ITS REPLACEMENT BY A MORE THOROUGH EXPLORATION OF BRITISH ARCHITECTURE.

Such romantic mythologizing was given added legitimacy by Georgian philosophers and aestheticians, who extolled the power of historical association as a means of enhancing one's response to architecture and the landscape and thereby improving one's taste and judgement. The Napoleonic Wars, as well, led to a curtailment of the Grand Tour of Europe and its replacement by a more thorough exploration of British architecture. And there was a growing sense that ancient houses and abbeys were fast disappearing. Travellers began to remark on the damage that encroaching industrialization was causing to older buildings, and journals of the time railed against the nouveaux riches nabobs who 'destroy the venerable mansions of antiquity, and place in their stead what seemeth good in their own eyes of glaring brick or ponderous stone'.

This is not to say that polite society didn't remain primarily concerned with contemporary architecture. It did, of course, and given the choice between a mansion recently built by Robert Adam and a mouldering Elizabethan courtyard house or a crumbling castle, few would have opted for the latter. But the castle and the courtyard house represented something just as important in the psyche of the Georgian upper classes. They may never have been places where the majority of landowners really wanted to live – entertaining the neighbouring gentry, raising a family and running an estate – but they were fantasies in brick and stone, a means of hanging on to a long-past (and largely fictional) society in which everyone knew their place and life was more stable, more ordered and more secure.

They also conjured up images of an older, better set of values that harked back, in the words of one mid-Georgian writer, 'into ages that are passed, into

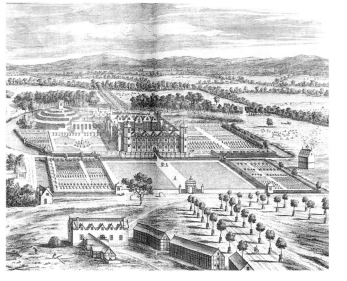

Dunham Massey in Cheshire: a memorial to a way and scale of living no longer possible.

the depths of the days of chivalry . . . the scene[s] of mirth and gallantry.' Like the romances of Scott and Byron, they provided an escape route, however temporary, into a safer world.

❖ ❖ ❖

The more uncertain and uncongenial the present, the more attractive the past becomes. By the later nineteenth century town dwellers, who from the 1850s onwards made up the majority of the nation's population, had to come to terms with the social effects of the Industrial Revolution in the shape of sprawling tenements and appalling urban squalor. They had also learned from Wordsworth, Coleridge, Keats and the Romantics who followed them that nature and the rural landscape had the moral edge, that 'To one who has been long in city pent,/'Tis very sweet to look into the fair/And open face of heaven'. Now people were being told

THEY CONJURED UP IMAGES OF AN OLDER, BETTER SET OF VALUES THAT HARKED BACK, IN THE WORDS OF ONE MID-GEORGIAN WRITER, 'INTO AGES THAT ARE PASSED, INTO THE DEPTHS OF THE DAYS OF CHIVALRY . . . THE SCENE[S] OF MIRTH AND GALLANTRY.'

by John Ruskin and William Morris that pre-industrial society was intrinsically superior to their own. The countryside and the past were two places where Victorians could be sure to find sanctuary from an unsympathetic landscape that was changing with bewildering speed. And where could they find those two ideals more perfectly expressed than in the serenity of the English country house?

Thus the scene was set for the twentieth century's love affair with the country house. The legacy of Romanticism is still with us, we continue to idealize country life at the expense of the city and cherish a hazy, make-believe vision of the past. We still regard mansions and manor houses as an ideal synthesis of history and rural life: 'There is a similarity of feeling at the root of the interest felt by the antiquarian and the lover of nature', wrote the conservationist Robert Hunter in 1907, 'both desire to perpetuate something which is apart from the life of the present.'

That turning-away from reality – and its links with the country house as an escape route – have been given more piquancy by the steady erosion of the landed classes' political power and lifestyle, with a dependence on armies of servants. Longleat 'is likely to prove a "show-place" of very wide appeal, a memorial to a way and scale of living no longer possible', said *The Times*, applauding the Marquis of Bath's decision to open his house to the public in 1949. This is surely still the key to so much of the country house's present-day appeal. The old order has passed, and we may or may not regret its passing, but we can still happily lose ourselves for an afternoon at Doddington Hall or Brympton d'Evercy or Penshurst Place, and forge a link with the past.

There's nothing wrong in that – so long as we remember that these visions of England, these links with the past, are simply interpretations, every bit as culturally conditioned as those of our ancestors. The value of such houses lies not in the attraction of the age that produced them – stunning though Penshurst is, who would really want to go back to the squalor and violence of the Middle Ages? – but in their safety, in their power to impart a vision of a lost Eden that we are secretly glad to have lost and that we can lose again by walking out of the great oak door and into reality.

The real reason why these visions are so precious is not because they are old or because – quite by chance – they have survived over time, or because they are memorials 'to a way and scale of living no longer possible'. They are precious because they are beautiful.

The Elizabethan house of Constable Burton was demolished in 1762, when, according to legend, its owner returned home from Scotland to find that his architect had misunderstood his orders to dismantle only part of the house.

'ONE OF THE CHARMS OF OLD HOMES IS THAT WITHIN THEIR WALLS ARE ENSHRINED MEMORIES AND TRADITIONS OF BYE-GONE DAYS.'

Thomas Colyer Colyer-Fergusson, one of Ightham Mote's many owners, in *Lady Hope, English Homes and Villages* (1909)

IGHTHAM MOTE
Kent

'Times change, and we change with them', wrote William Harrison in his 1577 *Description of England*. So too do houses, and Ightham Mote in Kent – already 240 years old when Harrison's *Description* first appeared – has changed more than most.

Standing for so long that nobody knows the name of its first owner, Ightham is an architectural style-manual in wood and stone. From its beginnings in the late 1330s, when it consisted of a single range containing hall, chapel, lodgings and kitchens surrounded by a wooden palisade – and the moat which gave it its name – each generation altered and extended it in different ways, according to the dictates of taste, fashion and fortune.

Today the palisade has gone, and the original hall wing, which stood opposite the entrance, has been joined by three more ranges dating from the fifteenth and sixteenth centuries.

An early Tudor gatehouse tower guards the bridge over the moat. There is a Jacobean staircase and Palladian and Gothick windows. The boards of a barrel-vaulted ceiling, painted with the roses of York, Lancaster and Tudor, may have once formed part of a pavilion set up when Henry VIII met Francis I of France at the Field of the Cloth of Gold. The walls of one drawing room are hung with eighteenth-century hand-painted Chinese wallpaper. And in the great hall, the sun shines through Tudor stained glass onto medieval roof timbers and late-Victorian panelling.

The result should be a disaster, a hopeless mishmash of conflicting styles and priorities. But somehow nothing jars, and Ightham Mote's integrity remains intact. Perhaps it is because each change is interesting in its own right. Or perhaps because those alterations tell us that Ightham may never have been a showplace, but it has always been a home.

Never a showplace, always a home – the Tudor gatehouse tower, with the medieval great hall opposite.

BRYMPTON D'EVERCY
Somerset

Most of Brympton d'Evercy dates from Tudor and Stuart times, but the buildings that combine with it to make such a perfect ensemble are rather earlier. Parts of the church of St Andrew date from at least the fourteenth century, the small dower house standing between them from the fifteenth century.

The dower house – if that is what it is, since it is also known as the priest's house – may have been built for Joan

Sydenham, whose father, John Stourton, gave the estate as a dowry when Joan married John Sydenham in the 1430s. The Sydenhams are largely responsible for the present appearance of Brympton d'Evercy. In the course of the sixteenth century successive Sydenhams built, remodelled and embellished the core of the house to the north and west.

Yet the chief glory of Brympton is the classical garden front shown in Knyff's view. Commissioned by the splendidly

The classical garden front at Brympton d'Evercy, commissioned by Sir John Posthumous Sydenham in the 1670s (Knyff, c. 1707).

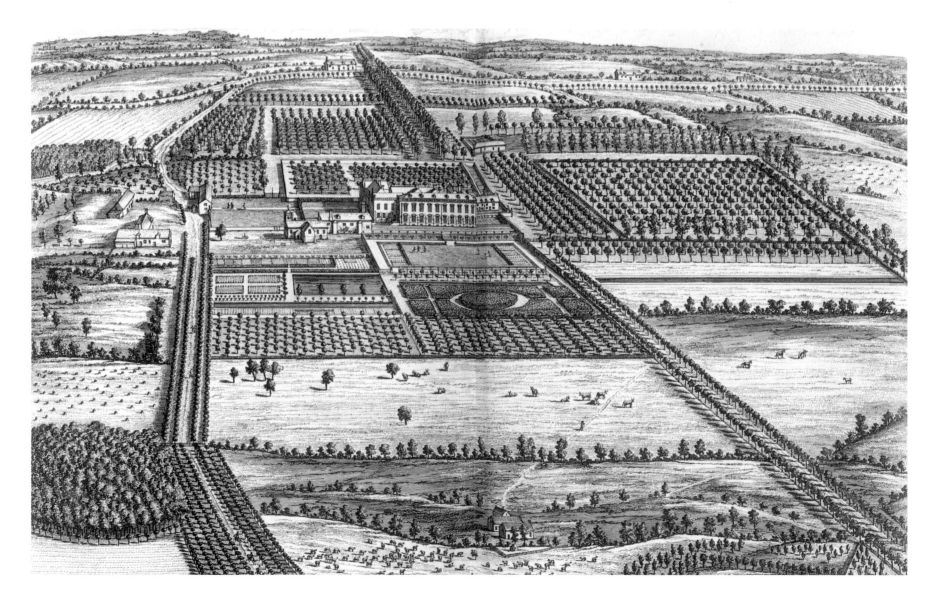

named Sir John Posthumous Sydenham in the 1670s, it consists of ten bays with low alternating triangular and segmental pediments on both the ground floor and the first floor, and a hipped roof behind a balustrade.

Considering its quality, its classicism and that it was constructed in the seventeenth century, it was perhaps inevitable that the garden façade should have been attributed at various times to Inigo Jones, notwithstanding the fact that he died two decades before it was begun. It is almost certainly a rare example of long-forgotten provincial masons borrowing from the Jones-Webb vocabulary of engravings or pattern books. Their confident handling makes one want to know their names.

By the time that Knyff's view was published, Sir John Sydenham's son Philip had decided to sell the family home, a

'Very large New Built Mansion, which had cost £16,000'. There were no takers, and the house was mortgaged to Thomas Penny, Receiver-General of Somerset, who most likely built the clock tower to the north-west. Penny was 'remiss in his returns to the Exchequer', and in 1731 Brympton d'Evercy was put up for auction, presumably to help make up the deficit. It was bought for £15,492.10s. by Francis Fane, a prosperous barrister.

The Brympton estate eventually passed to Francis's younger brother, who became the eighth Earl of Westmorland in 1762. In the early nineteenth century, the tenth Earl – the notorious 'Rapid' Westmorland – fell out with his wife, and she decamped to Brympton with her spinster daughter Georgiana. Georgiana, who lived there until her death in 1875, laid out the gardens we see today.

*Brympton d'Evercy.
Thomas Penny's clock
tower is on the left, and
Georgiana Fane's 'pond'
lies below the lawn in
front of the house.*

WHIXLEY

West Yorkshire

Knyff's view of Whixley Hall stands apart from most of his other work. There are no grand vistas here, no ducal palace to inspire awe and wonder. Christopher Tancret's modest red-brick house is a compact double-pile only seven bays wide, with projecting two-bay wings and a hipped roof – scarcely bigger, in fact, than the fourteenth-century church of the Ascension beside it. The gardens that surround the building are in keeping with this small scale, tightly packed together and soon giving way to parkland, while behind it to the north lies a complex of barns, stables and outbuildings, the appendages of a working farm.

But the scene still has an undeniable charm that is rooted in the simplicity of the landscape – the cattle grazing, the labourers making hay, the hounds trudging wearily home. The image is an idealized one, of course, but the impression that Knyff's view gives, and no doubt was intended to give, is of Whixley as a plain, honest house with no pretensions. One can picture Tancret's neighbours and friends hanging this print on their walls as a personal memento of their friend rather than as an advertisement of their political and social connections with a great man.

That feeling of simple integrity today is enhanced, if anything, by the lawns that have replaced Tancret's original garden layout. Architecturally, though, Whixley is something of a mixture. At its heart there is a building of *circa* 1620, but parts were remodelled in 1680, and the beautiful south front (shown in both the engraving and the photograph) probably dates from the end of the seventeenth century. The house was heavily restored by the Yorkshire architect Walter Brierley in 1907, presumably when the dormers were removed and the entrance altered.

A plain, honest house with no pretensions.

Whixley Hall by Knyff, 1707. Cattle graze, labourers make hay, and hounds trudge wearily home.

STANWAY HOUSE
Gloucestershire

Stanway is something of an enigma, with a building history that raises as many questions as it answers. At the Dissolution of the Monasteries, the estate, which had belonged for centuries to Tewkesbury Abbey, was bought by the Tracy family. To begin with, the Tracys probably modified the existing manorial buildings, which seem to have stood at the north end of the house (furthest away in Kip's 1712 engraving). In the 1580s they built, or rebuilt, the great hall and created the great sixty-light bay window that projects from its southern end. They also built, or remodelled, the south front to contain the principal lodgings, although all external evidence of this work has disappeared behind the present seventeenth-century façade.

Stanway's most famous feature, the elaborate gatehouse at right angles to the entrance front, was added around 1630. It stands three storeys high with three shaped gables, each crowned with the Tracy scallop shell. Although the concept of a heavily decorated gatehouse was becoming rather outmoded by Charles I's reign, its treatment is much more sophisticated than that of the Tudor house itself. The designer's name isn't known, but it may be the work of Timothy or Valentine Strong, members of a prominent Cotswold family of master masons and quarry owners whose work on Oxford colleges in the 1630s would have given them the necessary experience in Mannerism to produce the Stanway gatehouse.

'*TURNING A CORNER OF THE ROAD ONE COMES SUDDENLY UPON A WONDERFUL OLD GATEWAY WITH FANTASTIC GABLES AND A NOBLE JACOBEAN GATEWAY...AND OVER THE WALL PEEP THE GABLES AND ORNAMENTAL PERFORATED PARAPET OF A FINE MANSION OF CHARLES I'S TIME.'*

Allan Fea, *Nooks and Corners of Old England* (1911)

Kip's prospect of Stanway from the south, 1712.

*The northern range, by
William Burn, 1859-60.*

The authorship of the south front is also a mystery. It dates
from the late seventeenth century (a contemporary source
says that one wing of the house was unfinished in 1685 –
presumably a reference to the new range), but with its
strapwork cresting and mullioned and transomed windows, it
is as old-fashioned for its time as the gatehouse was modern.
It may even be that gatehouse and south front are part of the
same building programme, interrupted by the Civil War.

With the south front, Stanway was almost complete – but
not quite. The northern range, which contained service rooms
and domestic offices, was rebuilt in 1859-60 by William Burn
and enlarged in 1913 by the Arts and Crafts architect Detmar
Blow. Regrettably, most of his work was demolished in 1948.

*A perfect grouping of
church, house and
gatehouse.*

DODDINGTON HALL
Lincolnshire

Tall and austere, Doddington is strangely at odds with the rather unsophisticated gatehouse that opens onto the entrance court.

Doddington Hall belongs to a group of progressive country houses that appeared in the East Midlands during the last years of Elizabeth's reign, examples of which include Hardwick Hall in Derbyshire (1590-8), Wollaton Hall (1580-8) and Worksop Manor (completed 1586), both in Nottinghamshire. All these houses were designed by Robert Smythson, and it seems likely that Smythson was also behind Doddington. His client was Thomas Tailor, who bought the estate in 1593.

The house was completed by 1600 and, externally at least, has scarcely been altered since, save for the removal of the semicircular lunettes that adorned the parapet. Devoid of the flamboyant decoration that one associates with earlier Elizabethan houses – except for the single-storey crested Tuscan porch on the east front – it is uncomplicated and austere, strangely at odds with the fussy curved gables of the gatehouse, the relative lack of sophistication of which suggests it may have been designed by a different architect.

Knyff's early-eighteenth-century prospect of Doddington. The house has scarcely changed since it was completed in 1600.

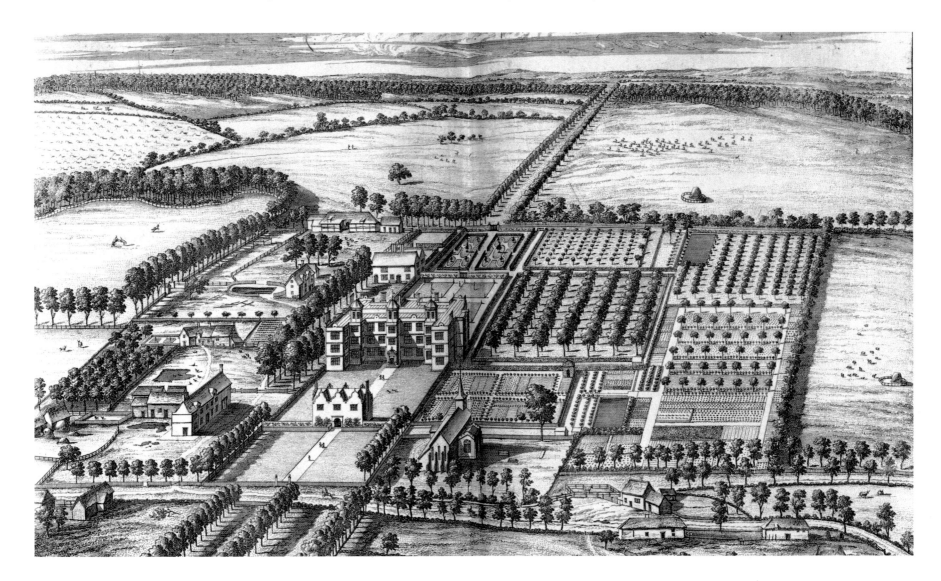

The main block is deceptively simple: an elongated H-plan with projecting entrance bays in the centre of both façades. The impression of height is accentuated by walls that are carried up above the eaves into solid brick parapets and by three octagonal turrets rising twenty feet above the east front, one over the porch and the others over the two square bays that stand in the angles of the wings.

The house passed in 1652 to the Hussey family, and after a period of neglect it was restored in the early 1760s for Sir John Hussey Delaval by the father-and-son partnership of Thomas and William Lumby, master carpenters of Lincoln. Thomas Lumby also rebuilt the little church of St Peter in a Gothic style, using Kip's engraving as a model.

In 1763 Sir John inherited the Delaval's main seat of Seaton Delaval in Northumberland, but by the terms of a family will he was barred from occupying both houses, and his younger brothers laid claim to Doddington. In a fit of pique he ordered that all the trees on the estate should be felled, only to find that his brothers were willing to settle – he lived out the rest of his life on a treeless and windswept estate.

The impression of height is accentuated by the walls, which are carried up above the eaves into brick parapets.

Doddington's severity has been softened by time. Before the red brick and yellow Ancaster stone mellowed with age, it must have been even more imposing, rearing up dramatically out of the flat Lincolnshire countryside.

120

GROOMBRIDGE PLACE
Kent

Groombridge Place was designed by an unknown architect for Philip Packer, whose father had bought the estate and its medieval house in the early seventeenth century. There is no precise date for its construction, but John Evelyn mentions two visits to the Packers – one in 1652, when the old house was still standing, and another in August 1674, when he noted that it was 'now demolish'd, and a new one built in its place'.

Stylistically it belongs to the late 1650s or very early 1660s. The hipped roof and dormer windows, the raised basement and the entrance façade's two projecting wings anticipate the compact gentry houses of the later Stuarts, but they disguise a house that is still essentially Jacobean in conception. Rather than being a fashionable double-pile with central hall and great chamber flanked by matching apartments, Groombridge is based on the traditional late-sixteenth- and early seventeenth-century H-plan, the crossbar of which is only one room deep. That room is the great hall (with a chamber above), and it is still entered at one end, rather than in the centre. Charming but cosmetic classicism in the shape of a single-storey pedimented loggia suggests that even before his new house was finished, Philip Packer was aware that fashions were changing. If so, his desire to keep up with the latest trends wasn't strong enough to prevent him from installing sixteenth-century panelling saved from the earlier building.

C. E. Kempe's romantic late-Victorian prospect of Groombridge, 'here represented in ye Reign of King Charles ye Second'.

Groombridge Place is much more than an intriguing example of a transitional architectural style. For one thing, it is an astonishing survival, having escaped any alteration – apart from the insertion of sash windows – since Philip Packer's time. Kempe's late-Victorian prospect, 'here represented in ye Reign of King Charles ye Second', is a rather fanciful reconstruction of the gardens.

Groombridge evokes a vision of England usually found only in guidebooks and advertisements. The warm red brick, the quiet waters of the moat and the way the house seems to grow out of the landscape all create a calm that fits perfectly with our rose-tinted images of the past. Dreams so seldom come true, and for this reason alone, Groombridge deserves a special place in the history of the English country house.

A vision of England usually found only in guidebooks and advertisements.

ATHELHAMPTON
Dorset

Rambling asymmetry and long lineage have made Athelhampton Hall a perfect candidate for the dreamy romanticizing that has characterized so much thinking and writing about the country house over the last two centuries – the sort of sentimental image-making epitomized by Joseph Nash's 1841 engraving, in which architectural detail provides a backdrop for scenes of life in the olden times. Nowadays we tend to smile knowingly at such a sanitized approach to history, but the irony is that no matter how one tries to escape into an earnest exploration of its architectural and social significance, an aura of romance still pervades and even defines Athelhampton.

The embattled hall wing dates from the end of the fifteenth century, when Sir William Martyn – whose family had been Lords of Athelhampton since around 1350 – obtained a licence to enclose a deer park and build a battlemented house with towers. Sir William's son Christopher added the parlour wing that joins the hall range at right angles. He may well also have been responsible for the circular dovecote that lies to the south-west. And some time before 1550 Robert Martyn contributed the gatehouse (to the left in Nash's print), aligned on the hall porch and dominated by a magnificent oriel window emblazoned with Martyn's arms and those of his wife, Elizabeth Kelway.

The Martyn line came to an end in 1595, and after changing hands several times the house was bought by George Wood in the mid-nineteenth century. Wood's new purchase was sadly neglected: part of the kitchen court had already gone, and the rest of the building was virtually derelict. Regrettably, he pulled down the gatehouse, but he also did a great deal to restore the house, as did subsequent owners.

A perfect candidate for dreamy romanticizing?

Rambling asymmetry and long lineage – Joseph Nash's 1841 engraving of Athelhampton, from The Mansions of England in the Olden Time.

'SYMPATHETIC RESTORATION MAY BE SEEN AT ITS BEST AT ATHELHAMPTON...NOT THAT THE HOUSE HAS BEEN MUCH ALTERED EXTERIORLY, BUT THE QUAINT OLD-FASHIONED GARDENS, WITH PINNACLED ELIZABETHAN WALLS, ANCIENT FISH-PONDS AND FOUNTAINS, HAVE SPRUNG UP AND MATURED IN A MANNER THAT HAD ONE NOT SEEN THE GARDENS AS THEY WERE, ONE WOULD SCARCELY CREDIT IT.'

Allan Fea, *Nooks and Corners of Old England* (1911)

PENSHURST PLACE
Kent

The fourteenth-century great hall, with its steeply pitched roof, stands at the centre of Penshurst Place. The church of St John the Baptist is in the foreground.

The earliest parts of the sprawling complex of buildings that make up Penshurst were constructed by Sir John de Pulteney, a wealthy draper and merchant who was Lord Mayor of London four times between 1331 and 1337. De Pulteney was given a licence to crenellate in 1341, and much of his house – a vast cathedral of a hall, the finest and most impressive example of its date still standing, with family lodgings in a first-floor solar reached via an external turret-stair – survives more or less intact at the heart of the present building.

The house passed to Sir John Devereux in 1382 and belonged from 1435 to 1446 to the Duke of Bedford, brother of Henry V. One or possibly even both of these men were responsible for a series of fortifications including the garden tower to the south, which was flanked by the curtain walls erected to encircle the house at the same time, and the great accommodation block attached to the south-west corner of de Pulteney's house. This is now known as the Buckingham Building, after the Dukes of Buckingham, who bought Penshurst in 1446 and retained it until the third Duke lost his head in 1521, at which time the house reverted to the crown.

In 1552 Edward VI granted Penshurst to one of his most faithful courtiers, Sir William Sidney, and it has remained in the family ever since. In the later sixteenth and early seventeenth centuries the house was extended by Sir Henry Sidney and his second son, Robert. His eldest son was the charismatic Sir Philip Sidney, the soldier-poet whose death at Zutphen in 1586 inspired more than two hundred elegies. Sir Henry built the long north range, which links with the Buckingham Building to the south and one of the towers of the late-medieval house to the west, and provided as its centrepiece the King's Tower, which replaced the old medieval entrance. In the early nineteenth century, sections of this façade were rebuilt in a Tudor-Gothic style by J. G. Rebecca. The formal gardens were laid out in the 1850s by George Devey, who used Kip's 1720 engraving as the basis for his scheme.

But such a stark list of names, dates and modifications simply does not do justice to Penshurst Place. Its appeal, enduring and almost painfully strong, has little to do with facts and figures, or catalogues of architectural alterations. Yet the precise nature of that appeal is much more difficult to define. But perhaps that is not so surprising – every country house is more than the sum of its parts. Architecture and landscape combine with personal and collective memory to

'THE FIRST VIEW WHICH I GOT OF THE OLD HOUSE OF PENSHURST...WAS AS I DESCENDED THE HILL OPPOSITE TO IT. ITS GREY WALLS AND TURRETS, AND HIGH-PEAKED AND RED ROOFS RISING IN THE MIDST OF THEM; AND THE NEW BUILDINGS OF FRESH STONE, MINGLED WITH THE ANCIENT FABRIC, PRESENTED A VERY STRIKING AND VENERABLE ASPECT.'
William Howitt, *Visits to Remarkable Places* (1838)

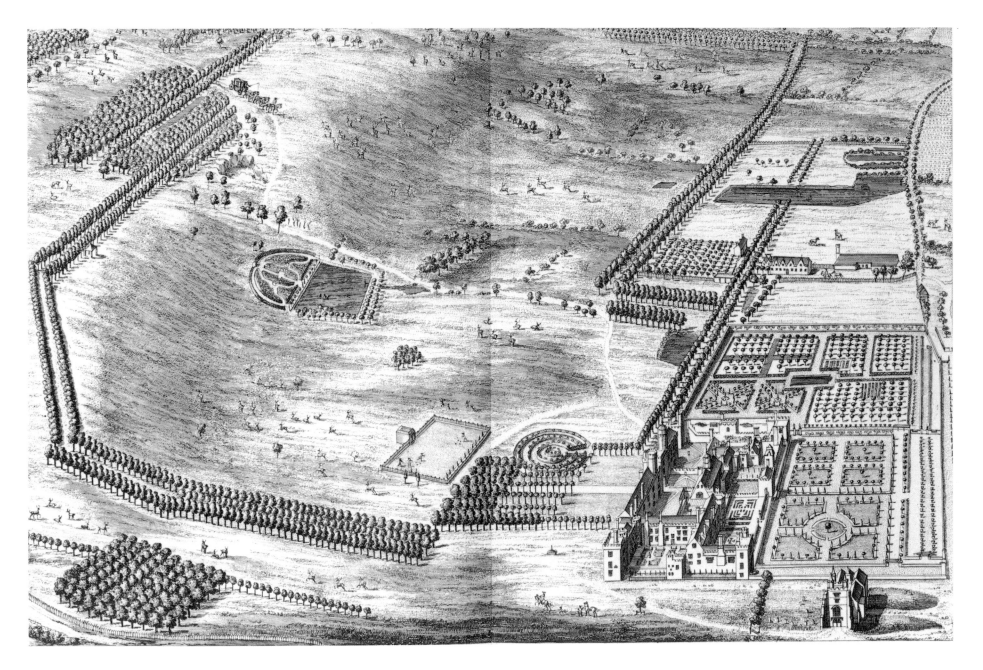

create something wholly unique, something that is at once an escape route into the past, an object of beauty, a scholarly treatise in stone. In a sense, the attraction lies not in the building itself, or even in the combination of cultural and historical elements, but in our experience of it, in the extent to which it meets or confounds our expectations.

Penshurst Place meets those all of those expectations and exceeds them. It is everything that a great medieval house should be: a rich mixture of old and even older, a home that has responded to the changing needs of generation after generation, and a symbol for our continuing love affair with the past.

Kip's 1720 engraving. When George Devey laid out the formal gardens in the 1850s, he used this view as the basis for his designs.

127

❖

'THOU ART NOT, PENSHURST,
BUILT TO ENVIOUS SHOW,
OF TOUCH OR MARBLE; NOR
CANST BOAST A ROW
OF POLISHED PILLARS, OR A
ROOF OF GOLD;
THOU HAST NO LANTHERN,
WHEREOF TALES ARE TOLD;
OR STAIR, OR COURTS; BUT
STAND'ST AN ANCIENT PILE,
AND, THESE GRUDED AT, ART
REVERENCED THE WHILE.'

Ben Jonson, 'To Penshurst' (1616)

❖

*Everything that a
medieval house should be.*

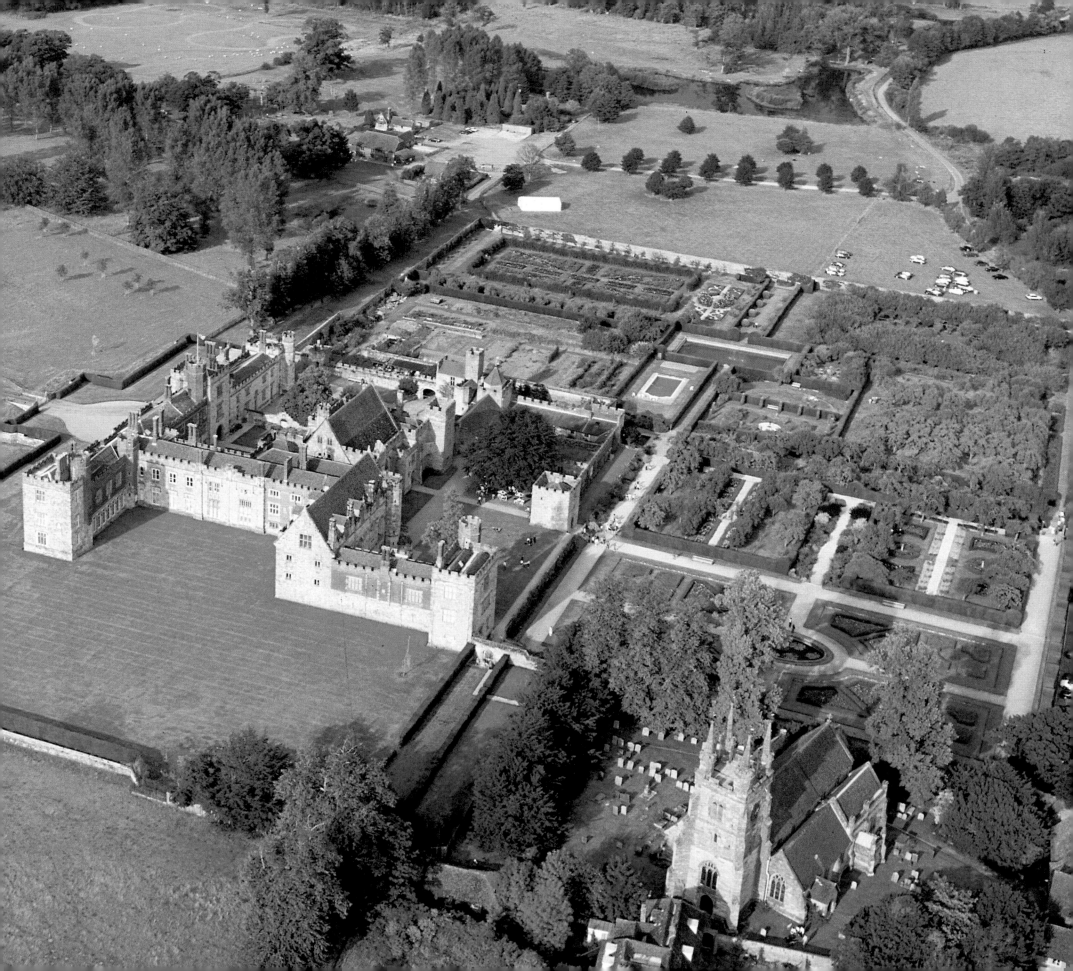

CHAPTER FIVE

If one of the most potent reasons behind the twentieth-century cult of the country house has been a sense of loss, a feeling that the social structures they express — with all their imagined stability and security — was passing away, then that sense of loss has been made more poignant by the realization that as those social structures were demolished, so too were the country houses. 'The large-scale private paradise is already obsolescent', wrote Clough Williams-Ellis in 1928. 'It is unthinkable that the great houses of England should be allowed to perish away.'

But the unthinkable was happening. By the end of World War I, a combination of falling land values and increased taxation meant that the estates that had funded the houses and lifestyles of their owners were

FORTUNE'S WHEEL

❖

CHANGE, DECAY AND THE
PASSING OF A LIVING
ARCHITECTURAL TRADITION

no longer viable, and estates were broken up and sold off. In 1918 the Earl of Pembroke sold off 8,600 acres, outlying parcels of the Wilton estate. The following year the Duke of Rutland sold half of his Belvoir estate, some 28,000 acres, and between 1919 and 1921 the Marquis of Bath reduced his Longleat estates by 8,600 acres. As the land was sold, so the country house that depended on it was often also sold. By 1920 *The Times* could lament, 'England is changing hands . . . Will a profiteer buy it? Will it be turned into a school or institution?'

Both of these things happened. Private schools did come to the rescue of many country houses. On the other hand, whole estates were also bought lock, stock and barrel by businessmen who sold off the agricultural

The romantic image of Bolsover has not been lost.

land in parcels and, if they couldn't get a good price for it, simply stripped the mansion's fixtures and fittings and demolished the shell.

A cable from the American magnate Randolph Hearst to his English agent in February 1924 ran: 'Are there any important ceilings to be had in England also staircase of Tudor of Jacobean period would like also one trussed ceiling of Guild Hall type Hearst.' There would have been no problems in fulfilling his requirements. Cassiobury Park in Hertfordshire, where John Evelyn had admired 'the divers faire and good roomes, and excellent carvings by Gibbons', was pulled down in 1922; the staircase now stands in the Metropolitan Museum of Art. Basildon Park in Berkshire, a beautiful neo-classical house built for an East India Company nabob between 1776 and 1783, stood empty for two decades before being offered for sale in 1928. There were no takers, but chimneypieces, doors, doorcases and plasterwork ended up in the Waldorf Astoria in New York.

While staircases and ceilings might find a resting place in San Simeon, New York or any one of a host of English houses that were, ironically, being 'restored' at the expense of their neighbours, the fact remained that some 460 country houses were demolished in Britain between 1918 and 1945.

Indignation at such wholesale destruction gained momentum during the 1930s and 1940s. 'Englishmen seemed for the first time to become conscious of what before was taken for granted, and to salute their achievement at the moment of extinction', wrote Evelyn Waugh in 1945 in *Brideshead Revisited*, that eloquent elegy to the stately homes of England. The result was a series of concerted campaigns by individual conservationists, private charities and eventually the state itself. In 1937, after an

TODAY THE BATTLE TO SAVE THE COUNTRY HOUSE IS ALMOST WON; BOTH THE STATE AND PUBLIC OPINION NOW RECOGNIZE IT AS A SIGNIFICANT AND IRREPLACEABLE PART OF OUR NATIONAL HERITAGE.

abortive attempt to mobilize country house owners to lobby for tax concessions from the government, the National Trust launched its own Country Houses Scheme, under which it was empowered by Act of Parliament to accept a country house, its contents and estate, together with an endowment in the form of land or investments to pay for its maintenance. In return, the owner and his or her descendants would be allowed to remain in the house as tenants. After World War II, Atlee's government created the National Land Fund out of the sale of surplus war goods as a 'thank-offering for victory', enabling the Treasury to compensate the Inland Revenue for money lost by the transfer of houses to the National Trust in lieu of death duties. And in 1950 the publication of Sir Ernest Gowers's report on *Houses of Outstanding Historic or Architectural Interest*, which concluded that 'we are faced with a disaster comparable only to that which the

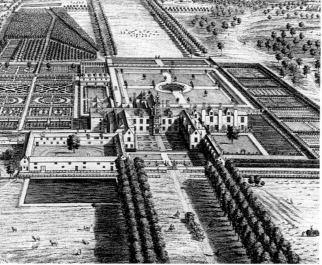

country suffered by the Dissolution of the Monasteries', led to the Historic Buildings and Ancient Monuments Act of 1953. Historic Buildings Councils were set up in England, Scotland and Wales to advise on the listing and acquisition of buildings of outstanding historic or architectural interest and to recommend the awarding of grants and loans towards their repair and maintenance.

❖ ❖ ❖

Today the battle to save the country house is almost won; both the state and public opinion now recognize it as a significant and irreplaceable part of our national heritage, and the debate has shifted towards a concern with the impact of modern architecture on the environment. Yet the passions aroused by that battle — the polemic, the angry denunciations, the public appeals — can easily blind us to the fact that an individual country house's continued existence has always been tenuous, that until the late twentieth centu-

Knyff's view of Brome Hall in Suffolk, the demolished sixteenth-century seat of the Cornwallis family.

ry chose, or was driven in sheer desperation, to pickle it in aspic, demolition and neglect and radical transformation were the norm. The suggestion that an Elizabethan magnate or a Victorian aristocrat didn't have the absolute right to do as he or she pleased with their own property would have been greeted with incomprehension. The Duke of Rutland didn't seek planning permission to replace his seventeenth-century home with a brand new castle in 1800. There were no letters of protest when the Grey family left Bradgate Park in Leicestershire to fall down in the 1720s, or when the Aubreys demolished Boarstall in the 1770s.

Take the buildings of Roger Pratt, one of the most influential architects of the seventeenth century. Kingston Lacy in Dorset (1663-5) was entirely remodelled in the 1830s. So too was Pratt's own home, Ryston (1669-72), between 1786 and 1788. The other three

PLANNING CONTROLS, LISTED-BUILDINGS CONSENT AND OTHER SUCH MECHANISMS ARE GOOD THINGS. WHAT IS NOT SO GOOD IS THAT CHANGE AS AN INTEGRAL PART OF COUNTRY-HOUSE ARCHITECTURE HAS ALL BUT DISAPPEARED.

houses that Pratt designed have also gone: Horseheath Hall, Cambridgeshire, was demolished in 1777; Clarendon House in Piccadilly (1664-7) stood for scarcely sixteen years before being sold to developers and then demolished; only Coleshill (1650-62) survived into the twentieth century in anything like its original form — it was destroyed by fire in 1952.

Perhaps Pratt was unlucky. But it is easy to think of other country houses — nationally important buildings, not drab Georgian villas or glorified farmhouses — that have suffered a similar fate. The great Baroque palace built for the Duke of Chandos between 1713 and 1725 and described by Defoe as 'the most magnificent in England' was sold on the Duke's death in 1744 and razed three years later. Wanstead in Essex (1713-20), one of the key buildings of the Palladian movement, did rather better: it lasted a hundred years before being pulled down.

So the list could continue, from major architectural works, such as the Smythsons' Bolsover, stripped of lead in the 1750s, to less important but still attractive buildings, like Brome Hall in Suffolk, a splendid sixteenth- and seventeenth-century house that has gone completely, to be replaced by a bungalow.

We regret these losses. No one who cares for buildings could fail to regret them, to wish that their owners had had more luck, or more taste, or more veneration for the past. But today we have another, less obvious cause for regret, a consequence of the mid-twentieth-century campaign to save the country house. Planning controls, listed-buildings consent and all the other mechanisms that prevent an individual from damaging our collective heritage are good things. What is not so good is that change as an integral part of country-house architecture has all but disappeared.

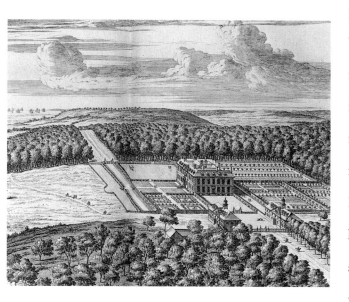

Until the present day, the spin of fortune's wheel has been a vital driving force in the development of the country house. If William Weddell had wanted to preserve Newby Hall untouched, we wouldn't have Adam's interiors. If the Earl of Dorset had felt our reverence for the past, Knole would have been the poorer for it. Half of Temple Newsam was demolished by a new owner in the seventeenth century. Wrest was completely rebuilt in the nineteenth. In fact, not one of the houses in this book has survived unaltered from the day it was first completed. But they all *lived*, they all responded to fashion and circumstance.

But now, barring the occasional accident, that is all done with. Fortune's wheel has come to a dead stop, and the country house, beautiful though it is, has become a museum piece. Its days as a living architectural tradition are over.

Burnt down in 1989, Uppark is being carefully rebuilt by the National Trust.

BOARSTALL TOWER
Buckinghamshire

A cartulary map of Boarstall in 1444. The fortified and turreted gatehouse is in the centre of the picture.

Built in the early fourteenth century by a powerful local landowner named John de Handlo, Boarstall must have once been quite a formidable castle. Surrounded on all four sides by a deep moat and set within a defensive wall or stockade, it probably consisted of a sprawling complex of buildings with a great hall at its core. The only access was over a drawbridge and through a fortified and turreted gatehouse.

Although no doubt modernized and altered to conform to changing standards of convenience and taste, Boarstall remained more or less intact until the Civil War, when many of the buildings close to the main house were demolished by Royalist defenders, so that they wouldn't be able to provide cover for Parliamentarian soldiers in the event of an attack. (The ploy was unsuccessful, and Fairfax's army took the castle in June 1646.) During the later seventeenth century, the old house was repaired and a series of formal gardens laid out. The eastern arm of the moat was filled in to form a long walk or terrace, while, externally at least, de Handlo's imposing gatehouse remained unchanged, except for the addition of a balustrade and bay window over the entrance arch.

It was a bowl of contaminated gruel, rather than the vicissitudes of war, that brought Boarstall's downfall. The gruel was eaten by the six-year-old only son of Sir John Aubrey, whose family had inherited the house through marriage at the end of the seventeenth century. His son died on 2 January 1777, and his heartbroken parents razed the house and moved away, leaving sheep to graze the gardens and farm labourers to live in the gatehouse tower.

Boarstall remained abandoned and neglected for nearly 150 years, although it continued to belong to the Aubrey family. In 1925 it was let to a Mrs Jennings Bramley, who lived in Florence but wanted a home in England. She put in electricity and water, created a new set of rooms from some old outbuildings adjoining the tower and brought over from Italy a man-of-all-work named Antonio Pinzani, who laid out a romantic garden to replace what remained of the Aubreys' formal terraces. Boarstall was given to the National Trust in 1943.

❖

'WHEREAS THEN [IN THE CIVIL WAR] IT WAS A GARRISON, WITH HIGH BULWARKS ABOUT IT, DEEP TRENCHES, AND PALISADES, NOW IT HAD PLEASANT GARDENS ABOUT IT, AND SEVERAL SETS OF TREES WELL GROWNE.'
Anthony Wood (1668)

❖

Abandoned and neglected for 150 years, Boarstall Tower was restored in the 1920s.

BRADGATE HOUSE
Leicestershire

Any ruined country house is a formidable repository of memories – ghosts who walked the broken galleries and crumbling halls and whose names are now forgotten. The Tudor mansion of Bradgate Park, which stands a few miles north-west of Leicester, has more memories than most, and many of its ghosts played major parts in the scrambles for political and religious power in sixteenth-century England.

The most famous personality is certainly Lady Jane Grey, who was born at Bradgate in October 1537, but there were others: her father, third Marquis of Dorset and Duke of Suffolk, who would be beheaded for his part in Wyatt's Rebellion eleven days after his daughter; Roger Ascham, later

secretary to Mary Tudor and Elizabeth I, who found Jane reading Plato while the rest of the household were out hunting; John Aylmer, Protestant Bishop of London under Elizabeth, who tutored Jane at Bradgate and introduced her to the works of radical German and Swiss reformers (several of whom also came to visit her here); and Bess of Hardwick, who may well have been in service as a gentlewoman-in-waiting to Jane's mother, the Marchioness of Dorset – she married her second husband, Sir William Cavendish, in the chapel at Bradgate shortly before embarking on her prolific building career.

The great house of diapered red brick was begun at the end of the fifteenth century by Thomas Grey, first Marquis of

Bradgate Park. Lady Jane Grey was born here and Bess of Hardwick was married in the chapel (View by Knyff, c. 1707).

'BRADGATE HAS BEEN DISMANTLED OF ITS TIMBER, AND ITS KEEPING, THO' NOT STOCK'D WITH DEER; AND THE HOUSE WAS LONG SINCE BURNT. IT WAS, I CONCLUDE, AND MIGHT BE RESTORED TO, I AM CERTAIN A NOBLE PLACE.'

John Byng, *A Tour in the Midlands* (1790)

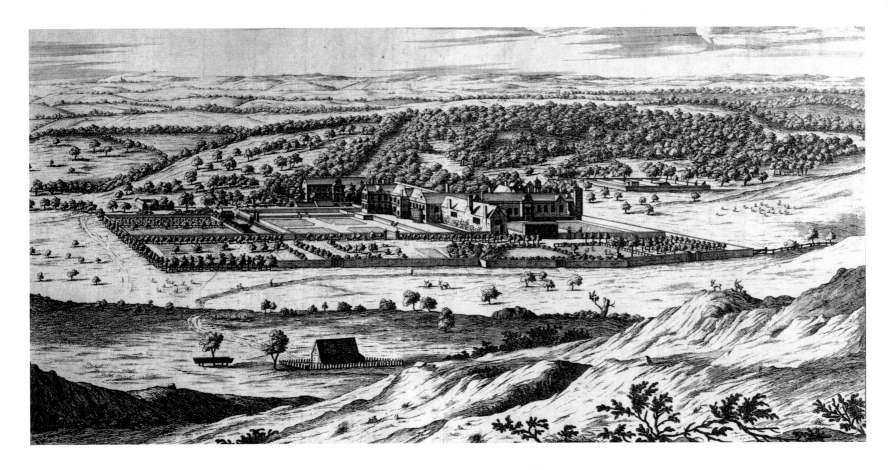

Enough remains to show what a spectacular mansion Bradgate must have been in its heyday.

Dorset. It was incomplete at his death in 1501, and it was left to the second Marquis, grandfather to Lady Jane Grey, to finish the U-plan building with a thirty-five-metre-long great hall and two projecting wings. The house was considerably extended – perhaps by Henry Grey, first Earl of Stamford – in the seventeenth century, when many of the buildings shown by Knyff were added.

After the death in 1719 of the second Earl of Stamford, the Greys abandoned Bradgate in favour of their other seat, Enville, in Staffordshire. The house then seems simply to have fallen down through neglect, although John Byng, who explored the ruins in the summer of 1790, speaks of it having been burned. What remains is enough to give a good idea of

Bradgate seems to have fallen down through sheer neglect when the Grey family went to live at Enville in Staffordshire.

the house, and several features, including the towers and the chapel where Bess of Hardwick was married, survive almost intact.

UPPARK
West Sussex

The Earl of Tankerville was a colourful character. In 1682 he ran off with his wife's eighteen-year-old sister, and at his subsequent trial was found guilty of 'the meanest duplicity, the basest falsehood, the most ungenerous, most ungrateful and most unfeeling selfishness'. A few months later he was implicated in the Rye House Plot and sent to the Tower. But it was late and the gates were shut, so he stayed up drinking all night with his guard until the poor man passed out and then simply rowed away to freedom and the Low Countries. He returned to England with Monmouth in 1685, commanding the cavalry at Sedgemoor so badly that he missed three chances to win the battle. Captured by James II, he turned King's evidence to escape execution and retired to the family estate in Sussex. There, having avoided James's command to repel William of Orange by pleading an attack of gout, he built himself a new house at Uppark.

Neither the date when Uppark was built nor the architect who designed it is known for certain. William Talman, who worked at Dyrham and Chatsworth, is the most likely candidate. We know from Celia Fiennes's description of the house that it was more or less complete by the time of her visit in around 1694. The house was 'new built, square, 9 windows in the front and seven in the sides, brickwork with free stone coynes and windows, itts in the midst of fine gardens, gravell and grass walks and bowling green . . . at the entrance a large Court with iron gates open, which leads to a less . . . it looks very neate and all orchards and yards convenient'. Her account corresponds closely with an early-eighteenth-century bird's-eye view by Knyff, although the stables and certain elements of the garden may well have been conjectural.

Tankerville died in 1701, and in 1747 his descendants sold Uppark to Matthew Fetherstonhaugh, who resited the stable and kitchen blocks to the north and installed a series of beautiful rococo interiors that boasted a magnificent collection of carpets, furniture and works of art, much of which was assembled on a Grand Tour between 1749 and 1751. After the Doric entrance portico was added by Humphry Repton in 1813, the house survived virtually untouched for more than 175 years, due in part to the fact that Fetherstonhaugh's son Harry became a recluse in later life, after marrying his dairy maid.

On 30 August 1989 Uppark was devastated by fire. Many of the contents were saved and the structure of the ground-floor state rooms remained intact, but the attics and first floor were gutted. In another age the building may well have been left to fall into ruin. But too many country houses have been destroyed over the last hundred years, and the least we can do now is to value the ones that are left. The National Trust, which has cared for Uppark since 1954, decided that the house's importance – both for itself and as the best setting for Fetherstonhaugh's collections – deserved a major restoration programme. This is scheduled to be completed in 1995.

Devastated by fire in 1989, Uppark is being painstakingly restored. Too many country houses have been destroyed over the last hundred years, and the least we can do now is to value those that are left.

An early-eighteenth-century view of Uppark, by Pieter Tillemans.

BOLSOVER CASTLE
Derbyshire

In 1608 Bess of Hardwick's youngest son, Sir Charles Cavendish, obtained Bolsover from his brother-in-law, the seventh Earl of Shrewsbury. By 1612 he had begun to convert the ruined medieval fortress, which had occupied the site since the twelfth century, into an impressive residence. But it was to be no ordinary house. In keeping with the spirit of the time, Cavendish and his architects, Robert and John Smythson, decided that part of the new building should take the form of a homage to chivalry, a romantic fairy-tale castle complete with towers and battlements.

The Little Castle at the northern edge of the site was the result. Enchanting and forbidding by turns, the high block with three turrets and a staircase tower, and the relatively low window-to-wall ratio, suggest that Cavendish was attempting a fairly serious revival of medieval forms that harked back to the fortified keeps of the early Middle Ages.

Knyff's early-eighteenth-century prospect of Bolsover, with the Little Castle to the left.

But however entertaining the Little Castle might be, Charles and his heir, William (who carried on the building work after Cavendish's death in 1617), also wanted convenience. Alongside the 'keep' rose up a large country house that contained a hall, lodgings, domestic offices and a great gallery within a huge range eighty metres long on a terrace to the south of the Little Castle. William Cavendish was a keen horseman, and an indoor riding school was added.

On 30 July 1634 Charles I and Henrietta Maria paid a visit to Bolsover as guests of William, by now the Earl of Newcastle. The house was still incomplete, a fact that was referred to in the masque that Ben Jonson composed for the occasion. *Love's Welcome to Bolsover* has carvers, masons, plasterers and glaziers, all presided over by Vitruvius himself. The prospect of further royal visits – the Earl was appointed

'IT MIGHT IN A FEW HOURS BE RENDER'D HABITABLE; BUT IT SURPRISES ME THAT THE DUKE DOES NOT GRATUITOUSLY OFFER IT FOR A RESIDENCE; WHICH SHOU'D ALLWAYS BE DONE WITH THESE OLD HOUSES. A SCHOOL WOU'D WARM IT WELL.'

John Byng, *A Tour in the Midlands* (1789)

The roofless terrace range once played host to Charles I: Ben Jonson wrote a masque specially for the occasion.

By the middle of the eighteenth century Bolsover had become a romantic ruin.

governor to Charles, Prince of Wales, in 1638 – led to further alterations, and between 1635 and 1640 the terrace range was remodelled and refurnished.

Then came the Civil War. Although Bolsover suffered during the Commonwealth, its present ruinous state is due not to Parliamentarian troops but to the architectural ambitions of William's own descendants. The family's principal seat was Welbeck Abbey in Nottinghamshire, and during the 1740s most of Bolsover's furniture and pictures were moved there. In 1751 the terrace wing was stripped to provide lead for a new wing at Welbeck. By the beginning of the nineteenth century the house that had entertained a King was the home of a suspended and rather shady vicar, who lived with his wife in the Little Castle.

'THIS CASTLE IS NOW
CONVERTED INTO AN
ILL-CONTRIVED
HOUSE; YET
SUFFICIENT VESTIGES
OF ITS ANCIENT
MAGNIFICENCE
REMAIN.'

William Bray, *Tour through some
of the Midland Counties* (1777)

The Little Castle was an
early example of an
attempt to revive Gothic
architecture.

DIDMARTON MANOR
Gloucestershire

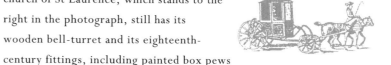

There is a pleasing ordinariness to Kip's engraving of early eighteenth-century Didmarton. Traffic moves steadily down the lane against a backdrop of rolling Gloucestershire hills. A coach-and-six drives past the little medieval church in the foreground, and riders gallop into the utilitarian court in front of the house. The grounds are formal, but not overpowering – certainly nothing to compare with the scale and magnificence of their Badminton neighbours. The manor itself is big, but not too big, and its gabled H-plan must have appeared to be of a bygone age when Kip's view was first published in the reign of Queen Anne. Didmarton was no Baroque showplace, crying out to be noticed and admired. It was a solid house of the late sixteenth or early seventeenth century, very much a gentleman's home rather than a nobleman's palace – and none the worse for that.

The landscape has changed surprisingly little since 1712, when Kip's view was published in Sir Robert Atkyns's *Ancient and Present State of Glostershire*, and Atkyns remarked approvingly on Robert Codrington's 'large House near the Church, with pleasant Gardens, and a great Estate'. The church of St Laurence, which stands to the right in the photograph, still has its wooden bell-turret and its eighteenth-century fittings, including painted box pews and a three-decker pulpit – the happy result of a Victorian decision to build a second church in the village rather than restoring the old one. The road still more or less follows its eighteenth-century route past neatly kept cottages to the north – although now of course it is cars and milk lorries that trundle along it rather than Robert Codrington's coach, or packhorses bound for the markets of Bristol or Tetbury. And it is still possible to see the vestiges of Robert Codrington's formal garden layout, with its gravel walks and curious statues, in the lawns and hedged compartments which lie to the south and west of the house.

The gabled core of that house still survives, too, although three centuries of change have taken their toll. The two projected wings that flanked the central block were demolished in the eighteenth century, when Didmarton was turned into a rectory and the Codringtons, who had acquired the estate through marriage in Elizabethan times, directed their attention to remodelling their principal seat at Dodington Park, five miles to the south-west. Rebuilt to the designs of James Wyatt between 1796 and 1813, Dodington was to become the grandest neo-classical house in the county, with a picturesque setting by Capability Brown and a plethora of garden buildings, including a dairy and bath house, a cascade and two impressive lodges. Didmarton, on the other hand, was left to its own devices, and in spite of – or even because of – its reduced scale, it still retains that homely quality which made it so attractive in Kip's day.

Kip's bird's-eye view of Didmarton Manor (1712) – more a gentleman's home than a nobleman's palace, and none the worse for that.

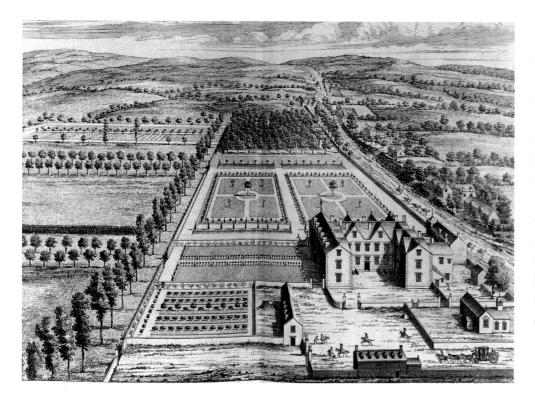

*Didmarton was shorn of
its two wings in the
eighteenth century.*

INGRESS ABBEY
Kent

Badeslade's engraving of Ingress is unusual among the historic prints and paintings in this book, but not because of the architecture. The asymmetrical ten-bay house fronting the Thames at Greenhithe is pleasant enough, but hardly remarkable. Nor are the formal gardens, which with their enclosed walks and parterres and avenues could have encircled any country house in the early eighteenth century, before William Kent 'leaped the fence and saw that

The Victorian Ingress Abbey is built of Portland ashlar, said to have come from the demolition of Old London Bridge.

all nature was a garden', in Horace Walpole's famous phrase.

What intrigues one most about Ingress is its setting. The arcadian landscape that usually surrounds houses of the period gives way at Ingress to a huge chalk pit, with smoke billowing up from a lime-kiln behind a processing plant or storage area. According to Daniel Defoe, lime was already a thriving industry along this section of the Thames by the 1720s.

Besides producing lime for building mortar, 'the rubbish of the chalk, which crumbles away when they dig the larger chalk or lime . . . is bought and fetch'd away by lighters and hoys' to be sold as fertilizer to the farmers of Essex, Suffolk and Norfolk. The proximity of the pits to Ingress suggests that its owner, Jonathan Smith, was both connected with them in some way, and proud of that connection.

Ingress was remodelled in the early 1770s for John Calcraft by William Chambers, who also built an elegant Doric temple in the grounds to display Calcraft's collection of Roman altars. But the temple was pulled down and re-erected at Cobham Hall in 1820, and Ingress itself was demolished by 1832. The Tudoresque building that replaced it was designed in that year by Charles Moreing for James Harmer. Constructed of Portland ashlar – said to have been recycled after the demolition of Old London Bridge – its gables, buttresses and battlemented central tower are dwarfed by the encroaching twentieth century in the shape of a vast paper mill.

❖

'LIFE IS FOR EVER CHANGING, AND DOUBTLESS EVERYTHING IS FOR THE BEST IN THIS BEST OF ALL POSSIBLE WORLDS; BUT THE ANTIQUARY MAY BE FORGIVEN FOR MOURNING OVER THE DESTRUCTION OF MANY OF THE PICTURESQUE FEATURES OF BYGONE TIMES.'
P. H. Ditchfield, *Vanishing England* (1910)

❖

Ingress in the 1720s, by Thomas Badeslade — chalk pits and lime kilns rather than the usual arcadian landscape.

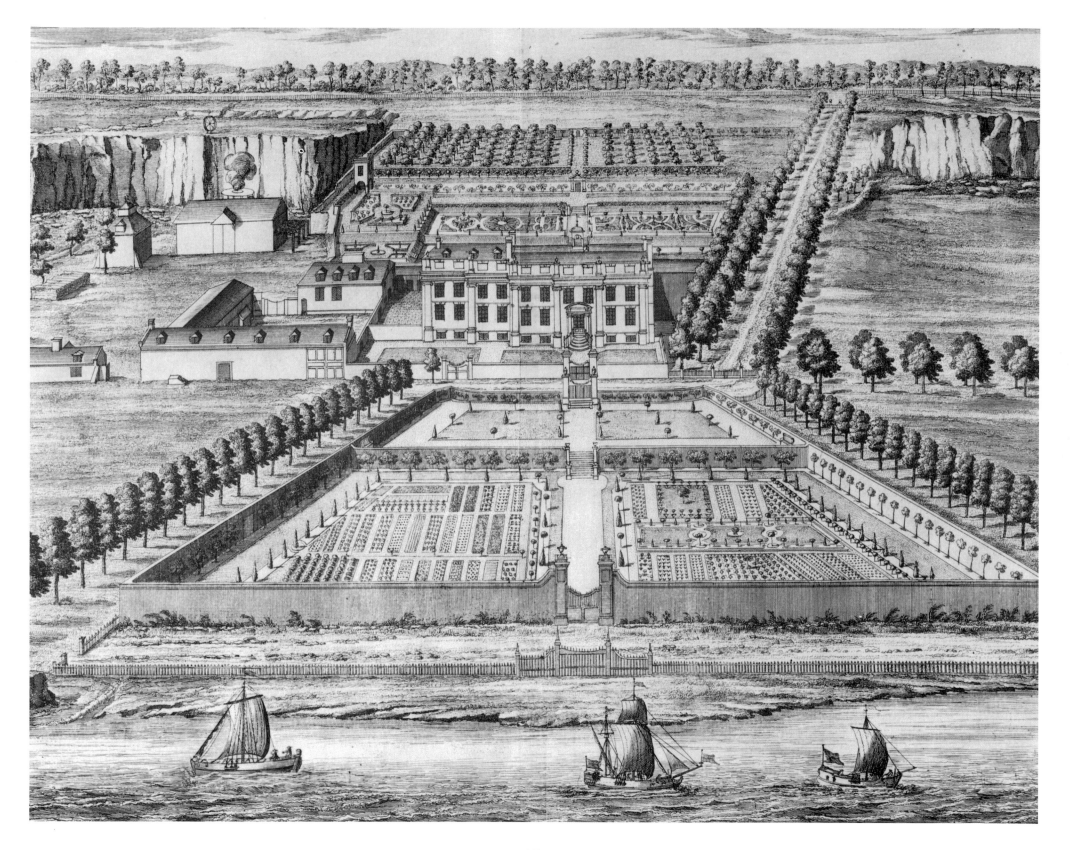

LEYBOURNE CASTLE
Kent

Nothing survives of William Saxby's Grange. The simple but attractive double-pile with hipped roof and dormers, its centre slightly recessed between projecting two-bay wings, has vanished – along with the scrollwork parterre, the formal gardens and the surrounding orchards. By the 1850s the Caroline house had been replaced by an uninspired Italianate villa designed by Samuel Dawkes that was destined for use in the present century as an isolation hospital.

Walter Godfrey's 1930 transformation of the ruins of Leybourne Castle – brutal, startling and innovative.

Saxby's other seat, Leybourne Castle, has a happier and more exciting past. Little is known of its early history. Badeslade's engraving shows a haphazard arrangement of lodgings and offices, possibly Tudor, and parts of a

battlemented curtain wall with two semicircular towers – the remains of a fourteenth-century fortified gatehouse with a portcullised entrance. In 1930 these remains were incorporated in a spectacular new building designed by Walter Godfrey, a well-known writer of scholarly pieces in the *Architectural Review*, whose sensitive and diligent restoration work at houses such as the Tudor Horselunges Manor (1925), Hellingly, and Herstmonceux Castle (1933) earned him a reputation as an equally scholarly architect.

A new Arts and Crafts vernacular house was grafted on to the remains of the medieval gatehouse.

But Godfrey's work at Leybourne is far from being a diligent restoration. Rather than attempting to rebuild the castle, as he did at Herstmonceux, he opted for a much more daring solution. A new, Arts and Crafts house was created to the south-east of the ruined gatehouse, more or less on the site of the twin-gabled block in Badeslade's view and directly grafted on to the medieval fragments, so that the curve of the eastern tower carries through into a concave gable on the new building. The effect is brutal, startling and innovative – as though the massive stones of the old castle were caught in the act of transforming themselves into something wholly new.

Badeslade's eighteenth-century view of the castle, with the vanished Leybourne Grange in the foreground.

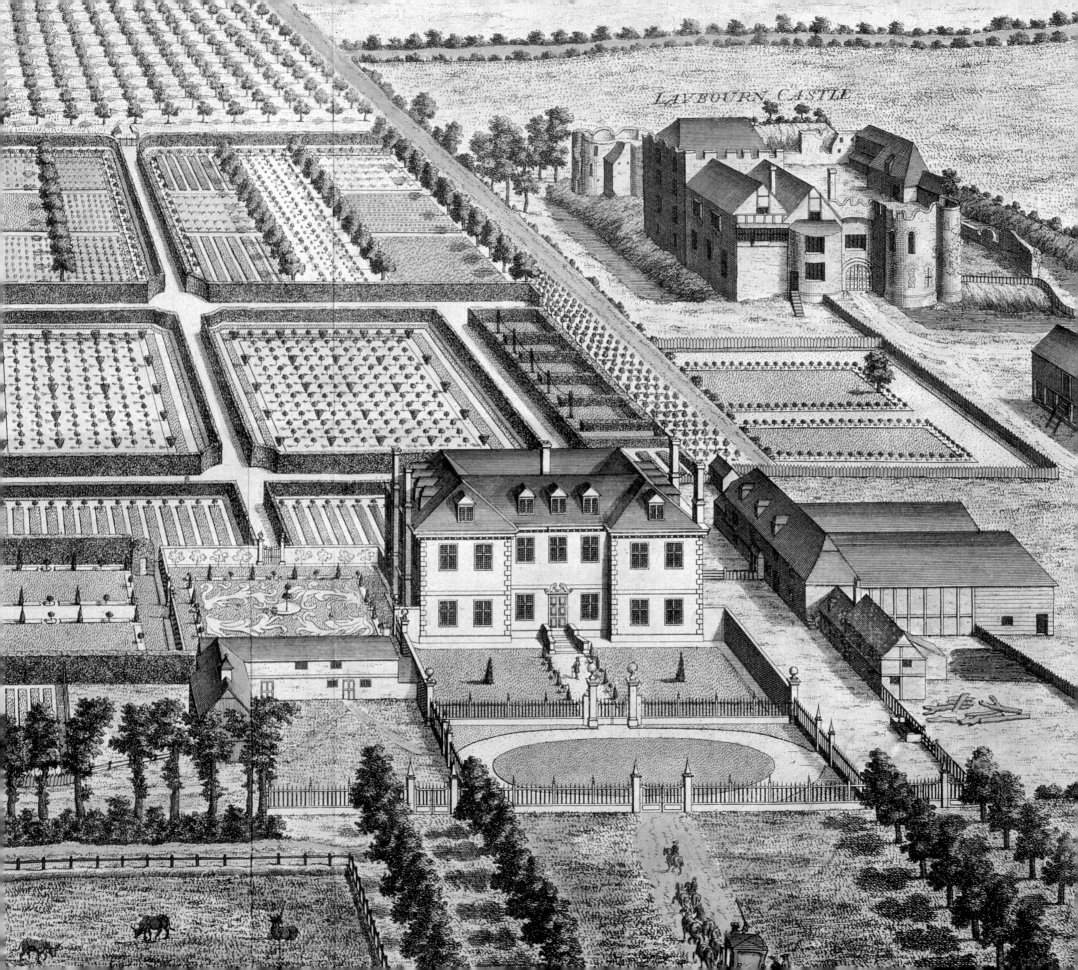

LAVBOURN CASTLE

LULWORTH CASTLE
Dorset

In spite of its battlements and turrets, Lulworth was never intended as a fortified house. From the first, the 'castle' was a plaything, an amusing conceit designed to evoke images from *The Faerie Queene* rather than to withstand a siege. It belongs to a small group of Spenserian fantasy castles that sprang up in the wake of the revival of chivalry at the end of the sixteenth century. Like Wollaton before it and Bolsover after it, the building's design toys with the idea of the castle, romantically reviving medieval forms in stone — just as its progenitor, the sham castle that played such a

'The lyttyll pyle yn Lullwourth parke', from a drawing by Mrs Humphrey Weld, 1721.

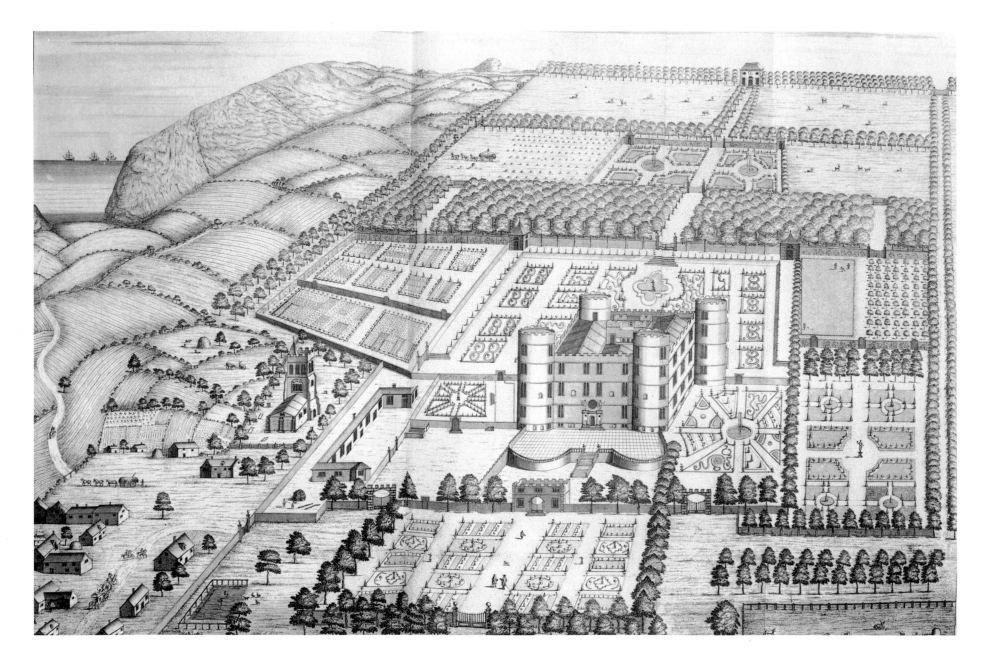

'THE WALLS OF
THE CASTLE
REMAIN VERY
LITTLE CHANGED,
BUT DANGER
NOTICES WARN
THE PUBLIC NOT
TO APPROACH
THEM CLOSELY
FOR FEAR OF
FALLING
MASONRY. TEA
GARDENS HAVE
BEEN OPENED IN
THE OLD ROSE
GARDEN.'
Pictorial and Descriptive Guide
to Weymouth, with special
notes for motorists (1947)

prominent part in Elizabethan pageants and tournaments, re-created them in pasteboard and wood.

The house was built circa 1608 as a lodge where its owner, Thomas Howard, could stay while hunting away from his main residence a few miles north at Bindon. The inspiration seems to have come from Robert Cecil, Earl of Salisbury, who was also creating a curious and faintly Gothic hunting lodge at Cranborne Manor in Dorset. In 1607 Howard wrote to tell the Earl about how 'the lyttyll pyle yn Lullwourth parke' was progressing, and to thank him for laying 'the fyrst foundatyon of the pyle yn my mynd' in a 'powrefull speche to me at byndon'.

The name of the architect of Lulworth is not known, although William Arnold, who worked at Cranborne, is a possible contender. Whoever was responsible for the design, the result of Salisbury's 'powreful speche' was an equally powerful battlemented block, about twenty-five metres square and three storeys high over a raised basement, with circular towers at each of the angles. The balustraded terrace shown in Mrs Humphrey Weld's depiction of the house was probably installed by her husband, whose family had bought the property in 1641. The Welds remodelled the house

Although it was built by Lord Bindon, the idea for a lodge in the shape of a castle at Lulworth seems to have come from Robert Cecil, who was creating his own curious hunting lodge at Cranborne in the early seventeenth century.

several times during the eighteenth century: John and William Bastard of Blandford Forum worked there from 1740 to 1758, and John Tasker, a Roman Catholic architect who worked chiefly for Catholic clients (which the Welds were), produced some impressive neo-classical interiors around 1780.

In the summer of 1929 Lulworth Castle was gutted by fire. For decades it remained empty and roofless, looking to all intents and purposes like a Gothick folly – more romantic, if less functional, in decay than it had ever been as a living house. It is currently being restored.

After a fire in 1929, Lulworth remained empty and roofless for decades.

Lulworth in the eighteenth century, painted by Bruyn in 1731.

INFORMATION BELOW ARE FOR HOUSES
OPEN TO THE PUBLIC. OPENING TIMES REFER
ONLY TO HOUSES (NOT GROUNDS) AND
ARE SUBJECT TO CHANGE. PLEASE TELEPHONE
AHEAD TO ENSURE THAT A GIVEN PROPERTY
IS OPEN.

Arundel Castle

Arundel

West Sussex

Tel (0903) 883136

*Open Sunday to Friday from April 1 to
October 29, 11:00-5:00*

Ashdown House

nr Lambourn

Oxfordshire

*Open from April to end October on Wednesdays
and Saturdays, 2:00-6:00*

Athelhampton Hall

Athelhampton

Dorset

Tel (0305) 848363

*Open Easter to October on Wednesday, Thursday
and Sunday, 12:00-5:00. Also open on Good
Friday and Bank Holidays, as well as Mondays
and Fridays in August, and Tuesdays from May
to September*

Audley End

Saffron Waldron

Essex

Tel (0799) 522399

*Open Tuesday to Sunday (and Bank Holidays)
from April 1 to September 30, 1:00-6:00*

Belton House

nr Grantham

Lincolnshire

Tel (0476) 66116

*Open April 1 to end October from Wednesday to
Sunday (and Bank Holiday Mondays),
1:00-5:30*

Belvoir Castle

nr Grantham

Leicestershire

Tel (0476) 870262

*Open April 1 to October 1 from Tuesday to
Thursday and Saturday, 10:00-5:00; Sundays
and Bank Holiday Mondays, 11:00-5:00*

Blenheim Palace

Woodstock

Oxfordshire

Tel (0993) 811325

*Open daily from mid-March to Oct 31,
10:30-5:30*

Bolsover Castle

nr Chesterfield

Derbyshire

Tel (0246) 823349

*Open daily from April 1 to September 30,
10:00-6:00; from October to end March,
Tuesdays to Sundays, 10:00-4:00*

Chatsworth

Bakewell

Derbyshire

Tel (0246) 582204

*Open daily from late March to end October,
11:00-4:30*

Chirk Castle

nr Wrexham

Clwyd, Wales

Tel (0691) 777701

*Open daily (except Mondays, Saturdays) and
Bank Holiday Mondays from April 1 to late
September, 12:00-5:00; open weekends in
October*

Doddington Hall

Doddington

Lincolnshire

Tel (0522) 694308

*Open from May to September (and Easter
Monday) on Wednesday, Sunday and Bank
Holiday Mondays, 2:00-6:00*

Dyrham Park

nr Bristol and Bath

Avon

Tel (027237) 2501

*Open daily (except Thursdays and Fridays) from
early April to late October, 12:00-5:30*

Groombridge Place

Groombridge

Kent

Tel (0892) 863999

*Open daily from early April to mid-October,
11:00-6:00*

Hampton Court Palace

Surrey

Tel (081) 781-9500

*Open mid-March to mid-October, Monday
(10:15-6:00), Tuesday to Sunday (9:30-6:00);
mid-October to mid-March, Monday*

(10:30-4:30), Tuesday to Sunday (9:30-4:30)

Ightham Mote
Ivy Hatch
Kent
Tel (0732) 810378
Open from April to end October on Mondays, Wednesdays to Fridays, 12:00-5:30; Sundays and Bank Holiday Mondays, 11:00-5:30

Kensington Palace
Kensington
London
Tel (071) 937-5174
Open throughout the year (except December 24-6, New Years Day and Good Friday)

Knole
Sevenoaks
Kent
Tel (0732) 450608
Open April to end October on Wednesdays, Fridays, Saturdays and Sundays (and Bank Holiday Mondays), 11:00-5:00; Thursdays, 2:00-5:00

Longleat
Warminster
Wiltshire
Tel (0985) 844551
Open daily all year (except Christmas), Easter Sunday to September, 10:00-6:00; remainder of year, 10:00-4:00

Newby Hall
Ripon
North Yorkshire
Tel (0423) 322583

Open daily except Mondays (but including Bank Holiday Mondays) from April 1 to September 30, after 11:00

Painswick Rococo Garden
Painswick
Gloucestershire
Tel (0452) 813204
Open February 1 to mid-December from Wednesdays to Sundays, including Bank Holidays, 11:00-5:00

Penshurst Place
Tunbridge Wells
Kent
Tel (0892) 870307
Open daily from end March to early October, 1:00-5:30

Ragley Hall
Alcester
Warwickshire
Tel (0789) 762090
Open Monday to Friday (and Bank Holiday Mondays) from mid-April to late September, 12:00-5:00

Stanway House
nr Broadway
Gloucestershire
Tel (038673) 469
Open from June to August on Tuesdays and Thursdays, 2:00-5:00

Temple Newsam
Leeds
West Yorkshire
Tel (0532) 647321

Open all year from Tuesday to Sunday (plus Bank Holiday Mondays), 10:30-5:30

Wilton House
Salisbury
Wiltshire
Tel (0722) 743115
Open early April to mid-October from Monday to Saturday, 11:00-6:00; Sunday, 12:00-6:00

Wollaton Hall
Nottingham
Nottinghamshire
Tel (0602) 281333
Open April to September on weekdays, 10:00-7:00, and Sunday, 2:00-5:00; October to March on weekdays, 10:00-dusk, Sundays, 1:30-4:30

Wrest Park
Silsoe
Bedfordshire
Tel (0525) 860152
Open from April 1 to September 30 on weekends and Bank Holiday Mondays, 10:00-6:00

Abbeys, Castles and Ancient Halls of England and Wales (n.d.)

Archibald Alison, *Essays on the Nature and Principles of Taste* (1815)

B. Sprague Allen, *Tides in English Taste* (2 vols, 1958)

W. Angus, *The Seats of the Nobility and Gentry in Great Britain and Wales* (1787)

Sir Robert Atkyns, *The Ancient and Present State of Glostershire* (1712)

T. Badeslade, *Thirty Six Different Views of Noblemen's and Gentlemen's Seats in the County of Kent* (n.d.)

John Bridgman, *An Historical and Topographical Sketch of Knole, in Kent* (1817)

Isaac Hawkin Browne, *An Essay on Design and Beauty* (1739)

S. and N. Buck, *Buck's Antiquities, Or Venerable Remains of Above Four Hundred Castles, Monasteries, Palaces…In England and Wales* (n.d.)

John Byng, *The Torrington Diaries, Containing the Tours Through England and Wales of the Hon. John Byng…Between the Years 1781 and 1794*, ed. C. Bruyn Andrews (4 vols, 1934).

Colen Campbell, *Vitruvius Britannicus* (3 vols, 1715-25)

Dr E. D. Clarke, *A Tour Through the South of England, Wales, and Part of Ireland, Made during the Summer of 1791* (1793)

Edward Conybeare, *Tourist's Guide to Cambridgeshire* (1892)

Daniel Defoe, *A Tour Through the Whole Island of Great Britain* (3 vols, 1724-6)

P. H. Ditchfield and Fred Roe, *Vanishing England* (1911)

Thomas Frognall Dibdin, *A Bibliographical, Antiquarian and Picturesque Tour in the Northern Counties of England and in Scotland* (2 vols, 1838)

John Evelyn, *Diary*, ed. William Bray (2 vols, 1818)

Allan Fea, *Nooks and Corners of Old England* (1911)

Celia Fiennes, *Journeys* (1983)

Laurence Fleming and Alan Gore, *The English Garden* (1979)

Benton Fletcher, *Royal Homes Near London* (1930)

William Gilpin, *Observations on the Western Parts of England, Relative Chiefly to Picturesque Beauty* (1798)

Mark Girouard, *Life in the English Country House: A Social and Architectural History* (1978); *Robert Smythson and the Elizabethan Country House* (1983); *The Victorian Country House* (1979)

J. Alfred Gotch, *The Growth of the English House* (1909)

S. C. Hall, *The Baronial Halls and Picturesque Edifices of England* (1848)

Charles G. Harper, *Mansions of Old Romance* (1930)

John Harris, *A Country House Index* (1979); *The Architect and the British Country House 1620-1920* (1985)

William Harrison, *Description of Britain* (1586)

R. Havell & Son, *A Series of Picturesque Views of Noblemen's and Gentlemen's Seats* (1823)

Oliver Hill and John Cornforth, *English Country Houses Caroline 1625-1685* (1966)

Historic Houses of the United Kingdom: Descriptive, Historical, Pictorial (1892)

Lady Hope, *English Homes and Villages* (1909)

William Howitt, *Visits to Remarkable Places* (1840)

Christopher Hussey, *English Country Houses Early Georgian 1715-1760* (1955); *English Country Houses Mid Georgian 1760-1800* (1955); *English Country Houses Late Georgian 1800-1840* (1955)

Gervase Jackson-Stops, *An English Arcadia 1600-1900* (1992)

Count Frederick Kielmansegge, *Diary of a Journey to England* (1762)

Nicholas Kingsley, *The Country Houses of Gloucestershire* (2 vols, 1989-92)

Leonard Knyff and Jan Kip, *Britannia Illustrata or Views of Several of the Queens Palaces also of the Principal Seats of the Nobility and Gentry of Great Britain* (1707)

Charles Knight, *Knight's Excursion-Train Companion* (1851)

Richard Payne Knight, *An Analytical Inquiry into the Principles of Taste* (1806)

John Henry Manners, *Journal of Three Years Travels* (1795)

James Lees-Milne, *English Country Houses Baroque 1685-1715* (1970)

William Mavor, *The British Tourist* (6 vols, 1800)

Joseph Nash, *The Mansions of England in the Olden Time* (4 vols, 1839-49)

J. P. Neale, *Views of the Seats of Noblemen and Gentlemen in England and Wales, Scotland and Ireland* (6 vols, 1818-23; 2nd series, 5 vols, 1824-9)

Arthur Oswald, *Country Houses of Kent* (1933); *Country Houses of Dorset* (1935)

Thomas Pennant, *The Journey from Chester to London* (1783)

Pictorial and Descriptive Guide to Weymouth, with special notes for motorists (1947)

Thomas Platter, *Travels in England 1599*, tr. Clare Williams (1937)

Uvedale Price, *Essays on the Picturesque* (3 vols, 1810)

Richard Pococke, *Travels Through England* (2 vols, Camden Soc, ns 42 and 44, 1888-9)

Mrs Philip Lybbe Powys, *Passages from the Diaries*, ed. E. J. Climenson (1899)

C. J. Richardson, *Studies From Old English Mansions* (4 vols, 1841-5)

William Brenchley Rye, *England as Seen by Foreigners in the Days of Elizabeth and James I* (1865)

Vita Sackville-West, *English Country Houses* (1941); *Knole and the Sackvilles* (1922)

Thomas Shadwell, *The Lancashire Witches* (1681)

Mary Sidney, *Historical Guide to Penshurst Place* (1903)

Henry Skrine, *Three Successive Tours in the North of England and Great Part of Scotland* (1795)

R. Strong, M. Binney and J. Harris (eds.), *The Destruction of the Country House* (1974)

Richard Sulivan, *Observations Made During a Tour Through Parts of England, Scotland and Wales* (1780)

Stephen Switzer, *Iconographia Rustica* (1718)

F. M. L. Thompson, *English Landed Society in the Nineteenth Century* (1971)

G. A. Walpole, *The New British Traveller* (1784)

Horace Walpole, *Journals of Visits to Country Seats &c* (1928)

Richard Warner, *Excursions from Bath* (1801); *A Tour Through the Northern Counties of England and the Borders of Scotland* (2 vols, 1802)

W. Watts, *The Seats of the Nobility and Gentry in a Collection of the Most Interesting and Picturesque Views* (1779)

Clough Williams-Ellis, *England and the Octopus* (1928); *On Trust for the Nation* (2 vols, 1947-9)

Henry Winstanley, *Ground Platts, General and Particular Prospects of all the Parts of his Majesty's Royal Pallace of Audley End* (n.d.)

J. Woolfe and J. Gandon, *Vitruvius Britannicus IV* (1767); *Vitruvius Britannicus V* (1771)

Adam, Robert, 54, 107, 135
Addison, Joseph, 52-3
Althorp, 26-27, 53
Anderson, MacVicar, 27
Anne, Queen, 13, 29, 52, 67, 104, 146
Archer, Thomas, 61
Arnold, William, 153
Arundel, 10, 12, 21, 40-41
Arundel, Earl of, 40
Arundell, Matthew, 90
Ascham, Roger, 138
Ashdown House, 10, 11, 15, 81, 94-95
Athelhampton Hall, 8, 10, 76, 104, 124-125
Atkyns, Sir Robert, 13, 146
Aubrey, Sir John, 34, 70, 136
Audley End, 10, 12, 17, 18, 30-33, 42

Bacon, Francis, 39, 104
Badeslade, Thomas, 14, 42, 58, 98, 148, 150
Badminton, 14, 19, 44-47, 104
Banckes, Matthew, 44
Banqueting House, 70
Basildon Park, 132
Bastard, John and William, 154
Bath, Marquis of, 109, 130
Beaufort, Duchess of, 14
Beaufort, first Duke of, 44, 46
Beaumaris, 58
Becket, St Thomas, 90
Beckford, William, 96
Bedford, Duke of, 126
Belton House, 80, 86-89
Belvoir Castle, 10, 11, 41, 80, 96-99, 130
Bess of Hardwick, 78, 100, 138, 139, 142
Blackett, Sir Edward, 54
Blandford Forum, 154
Blathwayt, William, 62, 63, 104
Blenheim Palace, 10, 15, 19, 20, 22-25, 52, 53
Blow, Detmar, 117
Boarstall Tower, 12, 134, 136-137
Boleyn, Anne, 40
Bolsover, 13, 130, 135, 142-145
Bourchier, Thomas (Archbishop of Canterbury), 36
Bradgate House, 134, 138-139
Bramley, Mrs Jennings, 136
Bray, William, 145
Bretby Park, 51
Brierley, Walter, 115
Britannia Illustrata, 13
Britannia, 14
Brome Hall, 135

Broome Park, 15, 42-43, 76
Brown, Lancelot 'Capability', 25, 35, 50, 53, 58, 73, 83, 100, 146
Brownlow, Sir John, 80, 86
Brympton d'Evercy, 109, 112-113
Buckingham Building, 126
Buckingham, Dukes of, 126
Buckler, C. A., 21, 41
Burges, William, 41
Burghley, 18
Burke, Edmund, 36
Burlington, Lord, 73
Burn, William, 117
Byng, John, 61, 96, 138, 139, 142

Calcraft, John, 148
Campbell, Colen, 19
Canons, 52
Canter, James, 40
Cardiff Castle, 41
Carlisle, Earl of, 10
Caroline of Anspach, 29
Carpenter, Edmund, 80
Cassiobury Park, 132
Castle Drogo, 21
Castle Howard, 10, 15, 20, 79, 104
Cavendish, Sir Charles, 142
Cavendish, Sir William (fourth Earl of Devonshire), 100, 138
Cecil, Robert, 153
Cecil, William, 79, 82
Chambers, William, 148
Charles I, 67, 70, 116, 142
Charles II, 30, 33, 44, 51
Charles, Prince of Wales, 143
Chatsworth, 10, 13, 15, 42, 51, 52, 53, 76, 79, 81, 100-103, 104, 140
Chesterfield, Earl of, 51
Child, Sir Richard, 20
Chirk Castle, 58-59
Clarendon House, 86, 134
Clarendon, Earl of, 86
Clark, Dr E. D., 70
Cobham Hall, 148
Codrington, Robert, 146
Coleshill, 134
Constable Burton, 109
Conway, first Earl of, 35
Coppin, Sir George, 29
Country Houses Scheme, 133
Cranborne Manor, 153
Craven, Earl of, 81, 95

Daniell, William, 40
Darnley, Lord, 72
Dawkes, Samuel, 150
de Caus, Isaac, 70-71
de Cort, Hendrick, 39
de Handlo, John, 136
de Montgomery, Roger, 40
de Pulteney, Sir John, 10, 126
de Vries, Vredeman, 90
Defoe, Daniel, 15, 19, 24, 29, 92, 134, 148
Delaval, Sir John Hussey, 120
Denham, Sir John, 78
Devereux, Sir John, 126
Devey, George, 126
Devonshire, Dukes of, 76, 79, 81
Devonshire, Earl of, 100
Dickinson, Lord, 68
Didbin, Rev. T. F., 99
Didmarton Manor, 146-147
Ditchfield, P. H., 148
Dixwell, Sir Basil, 42
Doddington Hall, 109, 118-121
Dorset, Earl of, 135
Dorset, Marchioness of, 138
Dorset, Marquis of, 138
Drewe, Julius, 21
du Cerceau, Jacques Androuet, 90
Dunham Massey, 13, 107
Dutch House, 42
Dyrham Park, 14, 62-65, 140

Eddystone Lighthouse, 12
Edward VI, 67, 126
Elizabeth of Bohemia, 95
Elizabeth I, 39, 58, 138
Emes, William, 58
Enville, 139
Etty, William, of York, 73
Evelyn, John, 26, 35, 70, 122, 132

Faerie Queene, The, 152
Fane, Francis, 113
Fea, Allan, 113, 116, 124
Fetherstonhaugh, Matthew, 140
Fiennes, Celia, 14, 19, 29, 51, 54, 67, 70, 71, 102, 140
Finch, Sir Heneage, 29
Fitzalans, 40
Fonthill Abbey, 96
Francis I (of France), 110

Garrett, Daniel, 73
Gaunt, Adrian, 79

George I, 13, 19, 29
George II, 29
Gibbons, Grinling, 19, 44
Gibbs, James, 35
Godfrey, Walter, 150
Gorboduc, 36
Goudge, Edward, 80
Gowers, Sir Ernest, 133
Greenwich Palace, 51
Gresham, Sir Thomas, 82
Grey, Henry, 139
Grey, Lady Jane, 138
Grey, Thomas, 138
Grillet, Monsieur, 51, 52
Groombridge Place, 10, 11, 12, 15, 42, 76, 104, 122-123

Haddon Hall, 104
Hampton Court, 10, 29, 50, 52, 66-67
Hardwick Hall, 78, 119
Harmer, James, 148
Harris, John, 14, 39, 42
Harrison, William, 110
Hartfort, Sir Edward, 106
Hatton, Sir Christopher, 78
Hauderoy, Samuel, 62
Haughton, 13
Hawksmoor, Nicholas, 29, 78
Hearst, Randolph, 132
Henrietta Maria, 142
Henry V, 126
Henry VIII, 36, 40, 67, 72, 110
Herbert, Lord, 44
Herstmonceux Castle, 150
Hewitt, Sir Thomas, 78
Historic Buildings and Ancient Monuments Act, 133
Holdenby, 78
Holland, Henry, 27
Hooke, Robert, 34
Hopper, Thomas, 41
Horseheath Hall, 134
Howard family (Earls of Arundel and Dukes of Norfolk), 40
Howard, Katherine, 40
Howard, Philip, 40
Howard, Thomas (Earl of Suffolk), 30, 153
Howitt, William, 126
Hunter, Robert, 108
Hurlbutt, 35
Hyett, Charles, 68-69

Ightham Mote, 10, 12, 15, 104, 110-111

Ingram, Sir Arthur, 72, 73
Ingress Abbey, 148-149
Irwin, third Viscount, 73

Jackson, Benjamin, 100
James I, 29, 30, 72
James II, 26, 100, 140
Janssen, Bernard, 30
Johnson, Thomas, 73
Jones, Inigo, 20, 27, 70, 78
Jonson, Ben, 18, 106, 142

Keene, Henry, 106
Kelway, Elizabeth, 124
Kempe, C. E., 12, 122, 123
Kensington Palace, 52
Kent, William, 29, 46, 53, 148
Kielmansegge, Count Frederick, 33
Kip, Johannes, 13-15, 26, 36, 44, 46, 54, 61,
   62, 67, 82, 95, 116, 127
Kitchener, Lord, 42
Knight, 22
Knole, 8, 15, 135
Knyff, Leonard, 13-15, 26, 35, 44, 46, 54,
   61, 72, 73, 82, 90, 95, 102, 112, 115,
   119, 138, 140, 142

Lacy, Kingston, 134
Laguerre, 19
Le Nôtre, 51
Le Pautre, 61
Lennox, Earl or, 72
Leoni, 20, 61
Leybourne Castle, 14, 150-151
Lincoln Cathedral, 97
London, George, 51, 54, 83, 100
Longleat, 9, 15, 18, 52, 53, 79, 82-85, 109,
   130
Louis XIV, 24, 51, 52
Louis XV, 61
Lulworth Castle, 152-155
Lumby, Thomas and William, 120
Lutyens, Edwin, 21

Marlborough, Duke of, 22
Martyn, Robert, 124
Martyn, Sir William, 124
Mary Queen of Scots, 40
Mary Wynter, Mary, 62
Mary, Queen, 67, 72
Maurice of Orange, Prince, 95
Maynard, Alan, 79
Melton Constable, 48

Miller, Sanderson, 106
Monjoye, Peter, 73
Montagu House, 35
Montagu, Ralph, 35
Moreing, Charles, 148
Morris, Roger, 27, 71
Morris, William, 108
Mortier, David, 13
Myddleton family, 58

Nash, Joseph, 124
National Land Fund, 133
National Trust, 133
Newby Hall, 14, 52, 54-57, 135
Newcastle, Duke of, 13
Norfolk, Dukes of, 10, 40-41
North, Roger, 44
Northumberland House, 30
Norton, Thomas, 36
Nottingham Castle, 13
Nottingham House, 29
Nottingham, Earl of, 29

Oswald, Arthur, 42, 122

Packer, Philip, 122
Packer family, 11
Paine, James, 78, 100
Painswick House, 68-69
Palladio, Andrea, 20, 71
Paxton, Joseph, 100
Pembroke, fourth Earl of, 70-71, 130
Penrhyn, 41
Penshurst Place, 10, 11, 15, 76, 104, 106,
   109, 126-129
Pinzani, Antonio, 136
Pope, Alexander, 19, 22, 53
Popham Conway, 35
Powys, Mrs Lybbe, 71
Pratt, Roger, 34, 86, 134
Pugin, A. W. N., 96

Radnor, Earl of, 52
Ragley Hall, 34-35, 53
Raynham Hall, 42
Rebecca, J. G., 126
Repton, Humphry, 50, 83, 140
Reynolds, Joshua, 22
Rhodes, Joseph, 96
Robins, Thomas, 68-69
Rupert, Prince, 95
Ruskin, John, 108
Rutland, Dukes of, 10, 81, 96, 130, 134

Ryston, 134

Sackville, Thomas, 36, 39
Sackville-West, Vita, 8, 10, 12, 39
San Simeon, 132
Saxby, William, 150
Seaton Delaval, 120
Serlio, Sebastiano, 90
Shadwell, Thomas, 106
Shrewsbury, seventh Earl of, 142
Siberechts, Jan, 76, 84
Sidney, Sir Henry, 126
Sidney, Sir Philip, 126
Sidney, Sir William, 126
Smith of Warwick, 46
Smith, Jonathan, 148
Smith, Thomas, 82, 86
Smythson, John, 142
Smythson, Robert, 79, 90, 119, 142
Somerset House, 70
Somerset, Lord Protector, 82
Spencer, Lord, 26
Spicer, William, 79
Stamford, Earl of, 139
Stanton, William, 80, 86
Stanway House, 116-117
Stourton, John, 112
Strawberry Hill, 106
Strong, Timothy, 116
Strong, Valentine, 116
Suffolk, Duke of, 138
Suffolk, eighth Earl of, 33
Sulivan, Richard, 82
Sunderland, Earl of, 26
Swakeleys (Middlesex), 42
Switzer, Stephen, 14, 62, 64
Sydenham, Joan, 112
Sydenham, Sir John Posthumous, 113

Tailor, Thomas, 119
Talman, William, 62, 76, 100, 140
Tankerville, Earl of, 140
Tasker, John, 154
Taylor, Sir Robert, 78
Temple Newsam, 53, 72-75, 135
Teulon, W. M., 27
Tewkesbury Abbey, 116
Thomas (Earl de Grey), 61
Thomas, Lord Darcy, 72
Thornhill, 19
Thoroton, Sir John, 97
Thynne, Sir John, 79, 82
Tillimans, Pieter, 141

Tompkins, William, 16, 33
Tudor Horselunges Manor, 150
Uppark, 135, 140-141

Van Nost, 68
van der Rohe, Mies, 10
Vanbrugh, John, 14, 22-25, 34
Verrio, 19
Versailles, 51, 67
Vertue, 30
Vitruvius, 142

Waldorf Astoria, 132
Walpole, Horace, 22, 53, 106, 148
Wanstead, 11, 20, 21, 134
Wardour Castle, 90
Waugh, Evelyn, 132
Webb, John, 70, 78
Weddell, William, 54, 135
Welbeck Abbey, 143
Weld, Mrs Humphrey, 152, 153
Westmorland, eighth Earl of, 113
Westwood, 104
Whixley Hall, 10, 42, 114-115
Willcox, Edward, 80
William III (of Orange), 13, 33, 40, 62, 63,
   86, 100, 140; William and Mary, 29, 67,
   104
Williams-Ellis, Clough, 130
Willoughby, Sir Francis, 10, 90, 104
Wilton, 27, 53, 70, 71
Wimpole, 14, 51, 52
Winde, William, 34, 80, 86, 95
Windsor, 41, 52
Winstanley, Henry, 12, 13, 30
Winter Queen, 81, 95
Wise, Henry, 29, 51, 54, 83
Wittgenstein, Ludwig, 11
Woburn Abbey, 70
Wollaton Hall, 10, 12, 15, 18, 77, 78, 81,
   90-93, 119
Wood, Anthony, 136
Wood, George, 124
Worksop Manor, 119
Worlidge, John, 48, 52
Wren, Sir Christopher, 18, 29, 34, 44, 67,
   78
Wrest Park, 53, 60-61, 135
Wyatt, James, 35, 41, 42, 80, 96, 146
Wyattville, 41

Yeats, William Butler, 104